FRANKLY
JUST BETWEEN US

My Life Conducting Frank Sinatra's Music

Published by Hal Leonard Corporation
7777 Bluemound Road
P.O. Box 13819
Milwaukee, WI 53213

Trade Book Division Editorial Offices
19 West 21st Street
Suite 201
New York, New York 10010

Library of Congress Cataloging-in-Publication Data

Falcone, Vincent.
  Frankly, just between us : my life conducting Frank Sinatra's music / Vincent Falcone & Bob Popyk.
    p. cm.
  ISBN 0-634-09498-X
  1. Falcone, Vincent. 2. Conductors (Music)--United States--Biography. 3. Sinatra, Frank, 1915- I. Popyk, Bob. II. Title.
  ML422.F33A3 2005
  784.4'8164'092--dc22

                    2005022446

Printed in the United States of America
First Edition
Book Designed by Hal Leonard Creative Services

7777 W. BLUEMOUND RD. P.O. BOX 13819 MILWAUKEE, WI 53213

Visit Hal Leonard online at **www.halleonard.com**

FRANKLY
JUST BETWEEN US

My Life Conducting Frank Sinatra's Music

Vincent Falcone & Bob Popyk

Hal Leonard books are available at your local bookstore, or you may order through Music Dispatch at 1-800-637-2852 or www.musicdispatch.com.

HAL•LEONARD®

DEDICATION

This book is in memory of Frank Sinatra, without whom none of this would have been possible; to my parents (also referred to as my "producers" by Frank Sinatra); to the girl who accompanied me on this journey, Connie Falcone; to my two sons Jeffrey and Daniel—two finer sons no man could ever have; and to Annette Falcone, who lifted me from the depths of despair.

It is also dedicated to musicians everywhere who want to make a career in music, and to everyone who wants to follow his/her dreams.

—Vincent Falcone

CONTENTS

ACKNOWLEDGMENTS

Many thanks are due to Nick Vaccaro of Syracuse, New York, for helping to come up with a title for this book; Cherie Yurco for her editing skills; all my friends at Local 369 of the American Federation of Musicians in Las Vegas; my friends at Local 78 in Syracuse, New York; the musicians I've worked with in New York and Los Angeles; and to my family whose tremendous support helped make my career possible.

I am grateful to Bob Popyk, a very gifted writer, entrepreneur, and gentleman, without whom there would be no book. And thank you to Hal Leonard Corporation for not only getting it in print but out to the public as well.

PROLOGUE

"Find a job you really like to do, and you will never have to work a day in your life."

Author unknown

It was at Caesars Palace, on the strip at the entertainment Mecca in the desert city of Las Vegas, where I realized dreams do come true. After years of playing piano in some of the worst places in the world, working at jobs I hated just to make a living, going to college, uprooting my family, and quitting a good-paying job just to see if I could make it solely as a musician, the hard work was really paying off. I remember it distinctly. It was Wednesday, January 3, 1976. I was at the piano. I was nervous beyond belief. The downbeat was about to drop. The curtain was going to go up, and I was going to be playing for "Old Blue Eyes" himself. I was the pianist at Caesars, up front with the "Chairman of the Board." I was in the orchestra, in front of a packed house, playing piano for one of the greatest legends of all time.

In spite of the moderate success I had already had in Las Vegas, I just knew this would propel my career as a pianist. After years of hearing how tough it is to make a living as a musician, I realized nothing would ever be the same after that night. I hadn't become an engineer, an accountant, or a marketing executive. I was a damn good piano player. I was earning a living playing at Caesars Palace and now for Frank Sinatra. Man, it doesn't get any better.

I think too many people today give up too easily on becoming what they really want in life. I am a firm believer that if you want to do something badly enough, there is always a way to do it. You just have to want it badly enough. Sometimes you have to give up a lot of other things to get where you want to go. There are risks. And with risks come rewards. I hate to hear someone say, "I can't." Usually what they are really saying is: "I don't want to."

Frank Sinatra was good for me, and I like to think, that in a way, *I* was good for *him*. I was his piano player, his conductor, and someone he could talk to. We went out to eat together. I had dinner at his house. I could call him on the phone. I was hired, fired, and rehired. I quit and came back. When I parted ways with Frank Sinatra for the last time, I went on to play and conduct for Tony Bennett, Andy Williams, Pia Zadora, Steve Lawrence & Eydie Gorme, Robert Goulet, Paul Anka, Eddie Fisher, Connie Francis, The McGuire Sisters, Al Martino, Jerry Lewis, Jack Jones, and many more great singers. What a great way to make a living!

Much of what I've achieved in my career I owe to Frank Sinatra. I have a lot to thank him for. He had confidence in me and gave me the opportunity to prove myself. That opened doors for me.

It was an incredible point in time, and each day I wake up and think how great it was. Every year was a very good year, the best was always yet to come, and it was "all or nothing at all."

♦♦♦

CHAPTER

1

What Am I Doing Here?

I can't remember when I didn't play the piano. I guess I started somewhere around the age of three. My mother was totally responsible for this. She saw to it that I had an excellent teacher and a decent piano (even though we could hardly afford it), and she also gave me my enthusiasm for music. My first teacher, Jane Notarthomas, was a friend of my mother and father who taught me to play by rote. I remember her spinning the piano stool up high enough so I could see over the keys, while my legs dangled two feet from the floor.

I continued to play through grade school, high school, and college, studying with Barbara Micale, a fantastically gifted woman. I would play for anyone who would listen. If no one would listen I would just play for myself. I loved it. The funny thing about it was, through all those years growing up, I never considered making a living at music. The money I earned from the bars I worked, the weddings I played, the singers I accompanied, and the shows I performed was supplemental income. I was taught that you had to have a real line of work. Being from a working-class Italian family, playing the piano was a hobby—not a job. You needed a "legitimate" career.

I grew up in Syracuse, New York. It's not the music capital of the world, but it's a nice place to be from and a wonderful place to grow up in. My mother's family emigrated from Italy, and they spent the rest of their lives in Upstate New York. I had four brothers, and we were a close family. When you live in one area most of your formative years, you don't know that the world is different from where you happen to live. You believe everyone has snow at Christmas. You get used to minus ten degrees Fahrenheit during the winter and expect the leaves to change into brilliant colors every fall. Back then I never thought that I would end up in Las Vegas, but it would have been something to look forward to. Some of those winter months in Central New York were killers.

It was natural to go to Syracuse University. I knew the area. I could play some of the clubs where I had become well known, make a few bucks, and get a decent education—something solid like engineering. Now that's a profession. I liked the whole idea of studying engineering because people could come up to me and ask, "What do you do?" and I could say, "I'm an engineer." My parents would be proud. My relatives would be thrilled. I ended up studying engineering at SU for two years. I hated it. I tried hard. I gave it my best. I was always good at math, but engineering just didn't do it for me.

So in my third year I switched to business administration. Now, I thought, I'm getting somewhere. Maybe someday I could run a successful business. Possibly I could be part of a major corporation. When someone came up to me and asked what I did, I could say: "I'm senior vice president at General Electric" (GE was big in Syracuse); or maybe even, "I'm chief operating officer at General Motors" (there was a GM division in Syracuse too). My parents would be delighted. My relatives would be happy. I would have a steady income, with three weeks of vacation every year, an eventual pension, plus medical insurance. It looked good on paper. In the end, I hated business administration even more than engineering.

I ran out of money in 1957. My parents had been support-ing my education as best they could, but I had four younger brothers and my parents had their hands full.

I took a year off from school in order to earn money to pay the tuition for the following year. Syracuse University's tuition back then was nine hundred dollars a year. (Now it's more than thirty thousand dollars!) I would work at General Electric as a material handler from seven a.m. to four p.m., then stick pins at a local bowling alley in the evening. On weekends I would play gigs in the Adirondacks and come back in time for work at GE on Monday. During that year of production line work at General Electric, I made up my mind that I would never end up in a job that I didn't enjoy. I decided then and there that when I returned to school it would be for music.

Through my piano teacher, Ms. Micale, I was invited to audi-tion for a music scholarship—which luckily I received. It made it possible for me to attend school without having to work on the side. I began to study music at Syracuse University in fall 1958.

I had been, up to this point, a student of classical piano. But the sound of jazz had begun to get into my brain. On my first day in the school of music I was looking for a practice room when I heard someone playing great jazz in one of the other rooms. I was numbed by the realization that this music I was hearing was what I wanted to play, but I didn't have the slightest idea how to play it. From that moment on, I decided that I would dedicate myself to learning how to play jazz. It has taken my entire life, and I am still learning.

For the most part I enjoyed the music courses at Syracuse University. They were easy for me because I have perfect pitch, which is the ability to hear any note and know exactly what it is. My parents discovered I had this talent when I was a child. You can hit two pieces of wood together and I can tell you if it's an A or G, or any note in between. Hit the side of a drinking glass with a knife and I can tell you the name of the note ringing out from twenty yards away.

This ability caused a rift with one of my professors. He taught a solfeggio class, where he would play recordings of string quartets and we would try to write down what we were listening to by ear. I was pretty much able to write what they were playing the first time around, then use the second time around to check for anything I may have missed. Then I would wait twenty minutes while everyone else tried to finish.

Once when we were doing this exercise, a pipe organ was also playing in the building. Hearing the organ and the string quartet recordings at the same time drove me crazy. I recognized everything I heard. I asked the professor to let me do the assignment when the pipe organ stopped. He told me I could hardly hear it and it couldn't possibly be getting in the way. I told him it was.

Kirk Ridge was another music teacher with whom I studied. He was a magnificent pianist and also had absolute pitch. I wanted the solfeggio teacher to ask him if he would have a problem with it. Professor Ridge concurred, and he told my solfeggio teacher that I had perfect pitch as well, and I was forever on the outs with the solfeggio instructor. I guess sometimes college teachers don't like to be wrong.

After two years of music school I decided that a degree in music would not determine whether or not I made it as a performing musician. The music courses at Syracuse University were becoming boring, and I felt I wasn't learning anything useful. The only thing that really kept me in school was studying piano with Professor Ridge. The days turned into weeks, then into months. I realized I had no passion for what I was doing.

On a dreary, depressing, gloomy afternoon in October 1960, I looked out the window of my car as I was driving home and said to myself, *This is nuts.* That was my last semester at college. In December I finally quit. I never went back.

CHAPTER

2

The Good, the Bad, and the Really Awful

After leaving the cobblestone sidewalks and ivy-covered buildings of Syracuse University in 1960, I just wanted to play piano, and I wanted to make a few bucks. To make it as a musician you need to play all kinds of places with all kinds of musicians. You need to network. So I started playing in several clubs and restaurants in the Upstate New York area.

Some places I played were great and paid well, and some were just a part of the learning curve. Each one represented an experience that helped me climb another rung of the ladder to becoming a professional musician. I had no lack of musicians to play with and places to play—places like the Coda, Luigi's, Lorenzo's with Bobby Doyle and Carl Mano, the Brown Jug, the Clover Club, the BelMar, the Casablanca, Drumlins (where we played jazz on Sundays), Three Rivers Inn owned by Dominick Bruno, Jazz at the Dinkler Motor Inn, Soo-Lin American-Chinese Restaurant, and Art's Townhouse. To end the night we would often go to Poodles & Jim's on North Salina Street for peppers and eggs at two o'clock in the morning.

A lot of great musicians came out of Central New York. They included Chuck and Gap Mangione, Sal Nistico, Nick Brignola, Sam Noto, Sy Simpson, Danny D'Imperio, Jimmy

Cavallo, Anna Marie Genovese, Calvin Custer, Tony Leonardi, Tony Riposo, and many more.

I grew up with Sal Nistico. We were childhood friends. Sal started out playing alto sax. He had so much in his head that he needed to get it out and get organized. When he played alto with our band, it was the worst we had ever heard. Of course, we weren't even in high school. We used to let him take one chorus and then tell him to sit down. What we didn't realize was that he was way ahead of us conceptually. When we were about sixteen, Sal picked up the tenor sax and left us in a cloud of dust. He eventually became one of the greatest tenor saxophonists ever, and one of the great stars of the Woody Herman band.

I started to make friends with the established local jazz players, most of whom were black, and they were all very helpful to me. I remember one night at the Embassy Club in Syracuse when I was asked to sit in with the group. The club was predominately black as was the group. They were always gracious to the up and coming musicians, black or white. After I finished playing, the saxophonist yelled out to me as I was leaving the stage. He said, "Man, you are *bad!*" Of course, being young and naive, I thought he was telling me how poorly I had played. I was crushed until one of the patrons explained that "bad" meant "good." In music, race was not an issue.

Besides piano, I started playing Hammond B-3 at Soo-Lin. I hadn't played the instrument on a job before, and with a lot of coaching by Sam Mancuso, an early mentor, I found my way around the keyboards. Also working there on Tuesday nights was Lyman "Butch" Strong, one of the best Hammond B-3 artists the world has never known. He should have received a lot more recognition than he has. A truly remarkable player, Butch is in a league of his own. He was a real inspiration and a great help to me.

My first road gig was with Gabe Garland's territory band. A territory band was a band made up of young guys who make little money and travel a particular territory doing club dates. It was a week here, three days there, sit around for a couple of days, and go someplace else.

I was paid seventy-five or eighty dollars per week with Gabe's band. When I asked for a five dollar raise I got it, but the trombone player took a five dollar cut to get it for me—there was no change in the total payroll. It was awful, the band was awful, and the places we worked were awful. But those are the dues you pay, and the experience you get, if you want to make a living playing piano.

Joe Carfagno, who is now secretary-treasurer of AFM Local 78 in Syracuse, used to play with the Gabe Garland territory band. I asked him what he remembered about the band. Here's what he recalls:

> *Gabe's band was not a small combo. It was a big band made up of twelve to fourteen members. I remember that for the last number Gabe had us dress as Mummers in these stupid feather costumes and march through the audience, or at least on stage. I don't think they were ever cleaned. Each night I couldn't wait to take a shower after getting out of the smelly parade suit. The piano player had to march playing an accordion. Vinnie had to do it too. This was definitely not a glamour job, but, hey, it was a job. And it was show biz.*

I could see that this road gig was a blind alley. I quit when we reached Philadelphia. I had had enough. I ended up back in Syracuse. When I wasn't playing, I worked at General Electric, parked cars at the Hotel Syracuse, and did a lot of menial things to supplement my income.

I continued learning about jazz and became obsessed with the idiom. I thought jazz was a great venue, and I was determined to learn how to excel at it.

My old friend, bassist Tony Leonardi, and I started playing together. At that time, Tony was a sax player. Sal Nistico was a schoolmate of ours, and we found ourselves playing together on many occasions. Tony and I started working in a black club in Elmira, New York called Berry's Hotel. There we met Eldon Brooks, who was a local singer. Man, what a voice! Eldon was really good.

The group was tight, and people seemed to like us. Tony somehow got us a gig which put us on the Holland American cruise ship, Groote Beer, that was doing a European cruise. The gig included some jazz concerts in Europe, and then a return cruise to the U.S. I fell in love with Europe. I also fell in love with a Belgian girl I met on the ship. She was an exchange student on her way back to Belgium after having studied in the U.S. for a year. The time went by like nothing.

At that age and time in my life, I thought things couldn't get any better. I knew that the music business was where I belonged. There was only one problem: sometimes the work didn't come in regularly, and I needed at least enough money to eat.

3

Food, Shelter, Clothing, and a Little Cash: Welcome to the U.S. Army

After returning to the States in early 1960, I found it very hard to find enough work to sustain myself, and I knew I wasn't yet good enough to move to New York or Los Angeles where the bulk of the work in music was found. I had to come up with another plan. It didn't take much thought. I enlisted in the Army.

I knew I was about to be drafted, and the Army was offering some incentives to join. One of them was the ability to pick where you would be stationed. I picked Europe. So, after six months of basic and advanced training at Fort Dix, New Jersey, I went back to Europe. I was sure with my musical background and ability, I would be assigned to the band. But no, after testing me the army decided that I had a talent for understanding Morse code. I guess my ability to hear rhythms made me good at code, and they sent me to Stuttgart, Germany. I was assigned to the Intelligence Corps, and shortly afterwards sent to Orleans, France, to join three other people stationed there.

As it turned out, I had one of the most interesting jobs in the Army. In those days, before satellites, we had operatives behind the Iron Curtain, and it was my job to communicate with them by code to gather intelligence. Because of the nature of my job, I was on call twenty-four hours a day, seven days a week. However, I was responsible to no one as long as I completed my duties. I wore civilian clothes, had a French car, and was given twenty-four-hour passes.

Between my assignments, I could go literally anywhere I wanted. On one of my 24-hour passes I met a man named Charlie Ralston, someone whom I will always remember. He was a government employee stationed at Orleans and an amateur drummer. He heard me play and immediately treated me as one of his family. We started playing together at the NCO and Officer's clubs in the area. It was great. I got to play piano, I had a lot of fun, and I made extra money.

One night when I wasn't playing, I walked into an NCO club to have a few drinks and hear the group there. I heard this male voice singing with the band, and I knew immediately that it was Eldon Brooks. Talk about coincidences and a small world. Nothing makes you feel better than running into people from home when you are thousands of miles away. Playing music with them makes it twice as good.

Charlie Ralston had some business smarts, and he got us booked at a jazz festival called Jazz au Chateau in a little Belgian town called Comblain La Tour. Joe Napoli, a former American soldier, ran the festival. He had been through the Battle of the Bulge, and he decided to live in Belgium after the war rather than return to the States

Here I was working for a fellow Italian-American in Belgium, with a singer from Elmira, New York. What a wonderful experience. It was like family. They loved Eldon, and we had the time of our lives. The festival was held in an old castle that had been used by the Nazis during the occupation. We were shown bullet holes in the walls of the castle where the Germans had executed resistance people. It was horrifying to see. Not a bad place to play, though—the acoustics were incredible.

Shortly after returning from Belgium, I was in Paris and walking down the Champs-Elysées when I saw a marquee advertising a two-night performance by Frank Sinatra. I wanted very badly to see his show, but I couldn't afford the price of a ticket. Sadly, I walked away. Fifteen years later, as Frank Sinatra's musical director, I told him that story. He looked at me and said, "Vinnie, you shoulda called me. I'd have gotten you a seat." The man had a hell of a sense of humor.

I went frequently to Paris in those days. I loved that city. It had all the things a young man could want—history, beauty, the Eiffel Tower, the Arc de Triomphe, the Louvre, beautiful girls, and, best of all, fabulous jazz. I would go to the many jazz clubs there at the time—Le Chat Qui Pêche, the Mars Club, the Club St-Germain, and others—and listen to the great American jazz artists who had chosen to live in France. They were all black men. At that time in our country's history, prejudice was still rampant, and black players had more than a tough time making a decent living in the U.S.

One good example was jazz pianist Bud Powell. He was beaten on the head by police in a racial incident. He never fully recovered and suffered from mental breakdowns. However, he was one of the greatest jazz pianists of all time, and played nightly at the Mars Club. I would go to hear him every chance I got. By that time in his life, he was really out of it from the drugs he had taken and hard living he had endured over the years. The club owner would lead him to the piano, and he would start playing and not stop until the club owner would go get him and tell him he should rest for a time. Bud would sit on a bench in the foyer and just stare into space. I would go sit next to him just to be near him. We never exchanged a word, but for me it was great. I felt it was time well spent. At times when he was playing, the old Bud would emerge for one or two songs. When that happened it was an education in playing jazz.

One night I was sitting in at the Mars Club, when Oscar Peterson and Milt Jackson walked in. I literally froze. I quickly took a break, and Oscar came up and played. What a night.

I've been back to Paris many times since those days. It's nothing like it was in those years, but I guess nothing ever remains the same. I was impressed with the European musicians' interest in jazz. The uniquely American genre of jazz was, and still is, revered by the Europeans and Japanese far more than it is at home.

During the time I was in Europe and in the Army, I met and became friends with many European musicians. The Dutch, at that time, were far and away the best of the jazz players. The Germans were too stiff, and the French were far too classical in their approach. That has all changed in the past forty years. Some of the European players are among the best in the world.

I loved being in Europe during that period of my life, but all good things eventually come to an end. I had had enough of the Army. When my enlistment was up, I was offered a commission to remain in the service, but I was eager to come home and pursue my career. I knew I was a musician, not a soldier. I returned to the U.S. in September 1963.

CHAPTER

4

No Great Gigs—
But No Uniform Either

When I came home from the Army in fall 1963, I started looking for work, but in Syracuse there wasn't much. A drummer friend called and offered me a job playing for strippers at a local theater called the Civic Follies. Having nowhere else to play, I took the job, which entailed playing a show every hour— with an hour off between shows, from ten a.m. to ten p.m., six days a week.

It was just the drummer and me playing the worst music you can imagine. Although there were obvious visual benefits, it was not what I was looking for musically. I will never forget having lunch and watching TV in a bar across the street from the theater on one of my breaks, when the news came that John F. Kennedy had been shot. I still had to go back to work. I couldn't play worth a damn after that, but it didn't really matter.

I renewed my friendship with Tony Leonardi. Because of a bad sinus problem Tony had converted from sax to bass, and we decided to form a group with Danny D'Imperio, a great young drummer from Cortland, New York, who became a life-long friend. The three of us started playing the clubs around Syracuse and we became quite popular.

At the time another friend of mine, Pete Procopio, had opened a club in Syracuse called the Clef. Pete was also a fine drummer, and Tony and I soon became a fixture at his club. It was here that I met Connie Dodson, who would later become my wife and the mother of my children. Tony was dating her roommate, and one night Connie and Tony's girl walked into the Clef, where Tony and I were playing. I knew the minute I saw her that she was the one for me.

Pete Procopio, former owner of the Clef remembers:

> *When Vinnie played, people were absolutely amazed at what came out of the piano. Everybody took notice, including the other musicians. Adele Durham who sang with us some nights at the Clef never had any charts or music of any kind. Vinnie didn't care. He could play in any key, transpose, or just find your key once you started to sing. Few piano players can do that. He is an exceptional talent. Vinnie was one of the best musicians to ever come out of Syracuse. Hell, he was one of the best musicians to come out of anyplace.*

Tony somehow booked the trio—along with a female singer named Marion Duke—into a club in Niagara Falls, Canada for several weeks. Tony's girlfriend and Connie came to visit us on weekends, and one weekend I asked Connie not to go back, but instead to stay and marry me. She did. The mayor of Niagara Falls performed the ceremony on April 2, 1964.

After leaving Niagara Falls, Tony got us booked into some real dives around Upstate New York. It was the best he could do and it kept us working.

Since memories can fade as years go by, I asked Danny D'Imperio how he remembered those days and those gigs. Here is his take on working with the trio:

> *That first gig as the Tony Leonardi Trio was on Christmas Day 1963 at a local Syracuse sewer called*

Luigi's. Luigi's was a pretty forgettable joint. (Except for a very funny gay waiter named Angelo who swished around the room taking drink and food orders.)

In all fairness, during the course of its existence Luigi's did manage to book a couple of major jazz attractions including Roland Kirk's band and the John Coltrane Quartet. We split the pay evenly among us. It came to seventeen dollars each per night. That engagement lasted a week.

Tony then managed to book us into an even more forgettable club (although much cleaner than Luigi's) called the Birches. The Birches was actually an East Syracuse restaurant. At Tony's urging they were willing to give music a try. The Birches gig lasted two weeks.

After the Birches, work for the trio was a little sparse, so we took a gig at Florento's Italian Restaurant in Brewerton, New York, with a local big band trumpet player named Guy Bono. Bono had been in the house band at Three Rivers Inn, which booked bigger national acts like Tony Bennett, Sammy Davis Jr., Bobby Darin, and Frankie Laine, so he had a few connections. For this gig, Bono took one of the dancers from the Three Rivers Inn chorus line and utilized her good looks and vocal abilities to enhance our performance. Marion Duke was sort of an Abbe Lane look-alike. Her voice was pleasant and she could swing. She was extremely easy on the eyes, and it's safe to say she really went over well with the crowd. This four-week gig paid ninety dollars a week. It was decent money back then.

Tony then booked us back into Luigi's with clarinetist Jack Maheu, one of the co-leaders of the Salt City Six, a popular Dixie group from Syracuse. Once again we were back at that elegant sewer. This time it was Jack Maheu with the Tony Leonardi Trio. With Guy Bono we had been just part of the Guy Bono Quartet, but now we shared billing!

After that, Tony obtained a contract from the Park Motor Hotel in Niagara Falls, Canada. We managed to get Marion on the job, voice unheard, as a result of her impressive promo photo. The initial contract called for four weeks, but the job was extended an additional five weeks, making the engagement a total of nine weeks. It was a six-night-a-week job with Sundays off. The first four weeks paid a hundred thirty dollars per week and the last five paid a hundred forty-five dollars. We were getting up there.

The final chapter of the Tony Leonardi Trio took place in a real mob-connected dump in Troy, New York, called The Riviera Club. It was six nights a week. We played from 9:15 p.m. to 2:45 a.m. and it paid a hundred forty dollars per week. The proprietor was a local tough guy named Jimmy "the Greek" Dabonis. To this day, I'm convinced that the only reason we got that booking was because of Marion Duke's promo photo. Music was not Dabonis's top priority. He wanted "flesh" on that stage and Marion Duke fit the bill perfectly.

By this time the trio was on thin interpersonality ice. At the end of sets I would disappear to a local gin mill next to the club to slam down a few in an effort to endure the increasingly unpleasant moments on the bandstand being generated by Tony's attitude. Though Vinnie was, and still is, not a heavy drinker, he would often join me in these attempts to escape. The first week, an undercurrent of dissent was brew-

ing and on our off night, Monday, the pot boiled over. For some reason Tony and I had words about the bad vibe going on in the group. Tony blew, as did I. It did not come to blows but it got real ugly. The Tony Leonardi Trio featuring Marion Duke had resigned itself to termination. We played together and Tony and I shared the same room. We just didn't talk. On the last day, I went to the room to get my bag and Tony was changing clothes to go out for breakfast. When he left I uttered the first words he had heard from me in over a week, "I'll see ya." His reply was, "Lock the door when you leave."

The Tony Leonardi Trio was no more. Neither Vinnie nor I ever saw or heard a single thing about Marion Duke again.

It amazes me how much Danny D'Imperio still remembers from dozens of years ago. Danny went on to play with the Glen Miller–Buddy DeFranco Band. He filled in for Buddy Rich when Buddy got ill. When we get together now, it's like I never left New York.

After the Riviera Club, Connie and I returned to Syracuse where I was offered a job playing piano at the Coda, which was owned by two fine men, Sam Traino and Norm Coleman. It was a godsend. They offered me a hundred and five dollars a week. I stayed there for quite a while and eventually brought Tony Leonardi in to play with me. It was a great learning experience for me. I would go listen to Tony Riposo and Billy Rubenstein, two excellent pianists from Syracuse. There was also a great singer in Syracuse, Anna Marie Genovese, who became one of my mentors and helped me learn how to play for a singer. Tony Riposo was musical director for The McGuire Sisters and also from Syracuse. One night at the Coda, Tony and The McGuires came in to hear Anna Marie while I was the pianist. That's how I first met the sisters, and years later I conducted for them on many occasions.

Syracuse was good to me. I met my wife Connie there. We got married and had two sons, Jeff and Danny. However, as I got older and my needs were greater, I realized I wasn't going to be able to make it financially as a working musician in Syracuse. I was playing piano six nights a week in a variety of local places and doing okay, but I knew I could do better.

CHAPTER

5

Priorities

When Connie and I returned to Syracuse from Troy, we needed to find a place to live, but our money was a little tight. I only had thirty-five dollars in my pocket and nowhere to call home. We found an apartment on the South Side for eighty-five dollars a month. I promised the landlady I would pay her the rest of the month's rent the following Saturday when I got paid by the Coda. She must have sensed my honesty, and she let us move in. I made sure I paid her as promised.

Having integrity is how I have always managed my career as well. Too many musicians today don't have their priorities straight. Punctuality, honesty, and credibility all play a part, just as talent does. You wouldn't believe the number of musicians I've worked with over the years who have an obvious disregard for professionalism. I have found that you get more work if you show up on time, work hard, and stand by your commitments.

One night at the Coda, a man approached me and introduced himself as Guido Singer. He was the owner of Clark Music and the most well-known music store in Syracuse. Guido proceeded to tell me that, although he thought I was a fine pianist, he was sure he could show me how to turn my talent into big money working for him as a piano and organ salesman. I thanked him and told him I wanted to continue my quest to be a full-time musician. He responded by telling me what a big mistake I was making, and that if I should change my mind, his offer was ongoing.

I loved playing at the Coda, but I was going nowhere fast. Connie and I had started a family, and I thought, what the hell, let me give this piano-selling thing a try. My only alternative to earn more money as a professional musician was to move to New York City, Las Vegas, or Los Angeles where the real music business was happening. At that time in my life, I didn't think I had what it took to compete in the "big time." So I went to work for Guido singer at Clark Music and found out in short order that I was very good at selling pianos.

Glen Donnelly, former manager of General Electric Credit Corporation (GECC) and now a Racing Dirt Track promoter, remembers:

Clark Music in those days probably sold more pianos and organs than the rest of the dealers in Syracuse combined. GECC was one of their primary sources for buying installment contracts, and I was branch manager at the time. Guido Singer was the owner, and he was as tenacious a marketing person as anyone I have ever seen. He was also a very intelligent man. Sales manager Jim Stanton couldn't play a note, and sold by sheer persistence and street smarts. Then Vinnie Falcone came along. He could play, and he was a genuinely personable guy, well-spoken, and sharp. Customers really took to him. With Stanton and Guido they were just customers. Vinnie had a remarkable way of selling to them and making customers his friends.

Fred Shoninger of Clark Music remembers:

When Vinnie started at Clark Music, it wasn't long before he became Guido's favorite employee. He just exuded personality, and never, ever looked shabby. Guido liked people with flair and talent, and Vinnie always dressed well, spoke well, and had a certain amount of confidence. He was polished, smooth, and had great delivery when he was selling pianos. It was easy for Vinnie to sell to anyone, because he had a knack for establishing instant rapport with people. No wonder Sinatra liked him.

I never thought I had a salesperson's personality, but I was successful. Clark Music had some of the better franchises back then, which included Hammond organs and Steinway pianos, along with stereo products. Marion Burke and Jim Stanton sold keyboard instruments and Fred Shoninger sold audio equipment. Fred's still there, but now, of course, he sells home theaters and plasma TVs. I actually liked the retail side of the music business. I had somewhat of a knack for selling pianos, and I could make sales without having to memorize fifteen different closes, to pressure people into buying, or having to be "slick."

I found that if you used some personality, believed in the product, could explain features and benefits, had a good demo, and asked people to buy, it was easy to make a sale. I could run rings around some of the other salespeople. Of course, the ability to play well helped in that line of work. There were other good dealers in Syracuse, so there was a decent amount of competition. A fellow in his early twenties opened up selling pianos and organs in North Syracuse, and he used to give us fits. He would do anything to get a sale, including bringing in an instrument from another dealer if he had to, just to grab a sale from us. Guido sometimes took it as a personal assault, but I took the attitude that there were plenty of customers out there that no one knew about. I wasn't going to reduce myself to being on the auction block, and therefore I always kept on a high road. It must have worked, because I became Guido's chief operating officer within two years, and I made more money than I had ever seen.

I was happy to be paying my bills. At the height of that career I was knocking down twenty-five thousand dollars a year. Man, that solved a lot of problems. Earning five hundred dollars a week was an incredible amount of money back then, and I still got to play gigs with my friends. I had a new car, a nice place to live, and could easily support my family. I also had a great place to work and a good boss, but I wasn't happy. I knew there was more life waiting for me out there. I knew I was first and foremost a musician, and that was how I really wanted to make my living.

CHAPTER

6

Enough Is Enough, I'm Off to Las Vegas

I labored for a long time over my decision to leave Clark Music in Syracuse, and all my playing buddies. I had made friends among both employees and customers. I even enjoyed going head-to-head with the competitor across town. I would see him on occasion when I played out on the weekends. He was younger than I was, and he also played a few casual gigs. I remember him coming into the Coda one night and hearing me play for the first time. He said it made him want to quit playing out and just stick with selling pianos and organs. At least he could give me a run for my money in that arena.

The owner of North Syracuse Music* remembers:

I recall going to the Coda where Vinnie was playing with some of the other guys from my store. We ordered a round of drinks and Vinnie sat down to play. I specifically remember him playing "Witchcraft" in five flats. My initial reaction was: This guy is in another league. He doesn't belong in Syracuse. It wasn't long after that night that I stopped playing altogether and just concentrated on the retail side of music. And it also wasn't long after that night that Vinnie decided to leave for Las Vegas.

*Editor's Note: The owner of North Syracuse Music at the time was Bob Popyk, co-author of this book.

I sold pianos to a lot of customers who encouraged me to move on in my musical career. Many became lifelong friends. Bill Rapp Sr., the owner of a Pontiac automobile dealership in Syracuse, was one of my biggest supporters, and he stayed in touch with me until he passed away. That's what is nice about making friends in a small city. For me the problem with being in a small city is that you can't achieve any major degree of success playing piano. And that's what I wanted to do.

Up to this point in my life, I had played more places that were really ratty gin mills rather than elegant establishments. I played because I like to play, and sometimes I couldn't be choosy as to where I found work. But I can tell you for a fact (and with all due respect to Billy Joel):

Sometimes the piano did sound like a carnival,
The microphones smelled like a beer
And people at the bar put money in my jar and said,
"Man, what are you doing here?"

I started asking myself the same question regularly. What was I doing selling pianos in Syracuse when I really wanted to play?

I think I made up my mind to quit my job and move to Las Vegas when I looked at myself in the mirror one morning. I asked myself if I really wanted to be selling pianos the rest of my life (which I liked), or if I wanted to take a shot at playing piano (which I loved) in the big leagues. Was I going to wake up one morning at the age of fifty and realize that I had not pursued my dream? I remember Jim Stanton at Clark's saying, "Your own decisions are your best decisions." I knew that, outside of discussing it with my wife, no one was going to make the decision for me.

Guido Singer thought I was crazy when I told him I was leaving to move to Las Vegas. He also had the means to make my decision a difficult one. He offered me a sizeable raise and a new car. He even offered to buy me a house. I still said no. He then offered me a piece of the business, which would have made me wealthy over a few years. I told him that, as much as I appreciated his generosity, I had to do this or my life would not be complete.

I met the owner of North Syracuse Music a few nights later at a local bar called Art's Town House. It was another place where there was live music, and I was there with my wife. He came over to where I was sitting at the bar, and I told him I had quit Clark's and was moving to Las Vegas to play piano. I don't remember his exact words, but they were something to the effect of, "Hey, are you nuts? You are making a ton of money selling pianos and organs. You can still play out whenever you want. Don't sell your house. You're going to be back. Mark my words. Remember this conversation. You will be back."

(Bob and I laugh about this today. I did come back to Syracuse, but it was many years later playing for Frank Sinatra, doing a show at the New York State Fairgrounds. He actually supplied the piano Sinatra used to warm up in his trailer.)

I quit my job, put my house up for sale, packed up my belongings, and took a deep breath before I headed west. I remember the feeling: I was scared as hell.

I had saved a few bucks so I knew we wouldn't starve. I also knew I would end up playing somewhere. Once I made the decision, I went to Las Vegas by myself in January 1970. I left my wife and two sons in Syracuse and drove out. I figured I would find some work and then have them come and join me. I felt like I was leaving a secure starting position with a triple-A ball club and going to spring training at a major league camp. I was either going to make it in the big time or I was going to be sent back down to the minors. When I left Syracuse, it was beginning to snow like hell, so I raced out of the state to avoid being caught in it.

I had to leave a car for my wife to drive in Syracuse, so my father-in-law let me borrow his 1969 Pontiac Firebird to drive out west. I figured I could make it to Las Vegas in three days if I pushed it. I was doing pretty well, and not exceeding the speed limit by enough to get me into serious trouble, when I ran into a snowstorm in Oklahoma like you wouldn't believe. I couldn't see three feet ahead of me. At times I was lucky to be going ten miles per hour. I didn't know whether this was an omen or not, and every once in a while I would think back to my warm house in Syracuse and the weekly five-hundred-dollar paycheck.

The snow got so bad I had to find an exit from the highway and a motel to wait out the storm. I found a little place right off the highway that reminded me of the Bates Motel from the movie *Psycho* and pulled in. By then, the snow had made the roads impassable. I asked if there were any rooms available, and to my relief found that there was one left.

When the clerk and owner saw my name, he asked if I had a relative who was in the Navy during World War II. He then showed me a picture of himself and his buddies from the Navy and pointed to one of the men in the picture. "That is Vince Falcone," he said. No relation to me, but what a coincidence. That coincidence kind of made me feel better and the thought of having to deal with an "Anthony Perkins" desk clerk left my mind.

The next day the sun shone brightly, the temperature rose to the low fifties, and I was once more on my way. I was anxious to get to Las Vegas. In the end it took two days longer than I had thought it would. Little did I know that *everything* was going to take longer than I thought once I got to Las Vegas.

The day I arrived in Las Vegas, the sun shone brightly and it was about sixty-five degrees. I knew I had done the right thing. I remember thinking to myself, one day you're going to be the house pianist at Caesars Palace. That was the goal I set for myself on that January day and I never wavered from that idea. Thanks to God, a lot of work, and a little good luck, I was eventually able to achieve my dream and beyond. I knew it would take a great deal of hard work and some good fortune. I worked as hard as I could and the luck followed. I never looked back once I left Syracuse. Las Vegas was where I wanted to be. But it certainly wasn't easy once I got there. Not in the least.

7

Getting By with a
Little Help from My Friends

I needed a place to live, so I rented a room at the Warren House motel, which is still in business today. Back then, it was behind the Flamingo; now it's behind the Imperial Palace. (The motel didn't move-the area got built up around it.) I was paying ninety dollars a week to have a place to temporarily call home, and I immediately started finding people to hook up with. I knew Pete Lulis, the house drummer at Caesars Palace, and guitarist Tommy McDermott, who was playing at one of the hotels on the strip with a relief band—they were both from Syracuse. I got them to introduce me to their circle of musician friends, and that was how I began to network.

I also went to the local American Federation of Musicians union hall and transferred my union card from Local 78 in Syracuse to Local 369 in Las Vegas. I immediately got to know many of the other union musicians there. Back then, James C. Petrillo was international AFM president. The union had three times as many members as it does today, and the rules were also a lot stiffer. The union had an induction period. There was a protective clause stating that any musicians transferring into Las Vegas from another local had to wait six months before taking a gig as a steady player. And you also had to wait three months before you could do even a casual date (single engagement). All the hotels were signatories, and the union and the hotels had a very good working relationship.

Mark Massagli was secretary-treasurer of Local 369 at the time, and he went on to become international president. It wasn't until after he retired that the transfer provision was removed. I asked him to comment about it for this book:

> *That transfer provision is no longer in place. It was a good thing back then, but things change. The music business has changed. I remember that Vinnie's colleagues held him in the highest regard...— both those he played with and those he conducted. I never heard anyone say anything bad about him, ever. That was really rare with the amount of musicians Local 369 had back then. There were some unique personalities, and every so often a few sparks would fly, but not with Vinnie. He let his playing do the talking for him.*

Local 369 had a rehearsal hall, and every night there would be something going on—jam sessions, practice sessions, and so forth. I would go there each night and try to meet more musicians, ask to sit in, and get them to hear me play. I knocked myself out trying to do the best networking I could. That, however, did not make me a living. I couldn't play a casual date for the first three months, and even if I could, those jobs were almost nonexistent. Gigs were few and far between for an unknown piano player from Syracuse, New York.

After living in Las Vegas for a month, Connie came out for a visit. We decided that we were not going to wait any longer, our family would move out as soon as possible. We would rent a house and live off our savings until I found a way to earn some income. I kept pounding the pavement, meeting people, and trying to network. I realized, once I got to Las Vegas, that it would be easier to get started with the support of my family.

A few weeks later my old boss Guido Singer called me and asked if I would come back there for a few days to help him out with an advertising co-op problem he was having. He offered to pay my airfare and to add an additional amount of money for my time spent straightening things out. Because I had already decided it was time to bring my family to Las Vegas, it was a great opportunity. I flew back to Syracuse, solved Guido's problem, packed up my family, and once more drove across country to start my new life. There were no snowstorms this time, and my family was with me. I thought my luck was beginning to change. But as I was going to find out, luck doesn't change overnight.

While I was working at Clark Music back in Syracuse, I had gotten to know John and Henry Steinway. They had become my friends. I thought I would look for tuning work through the local Steinway dealership in Vegas, and I soon found out the Steinways brothers had greased the skids for me. (They had actually called ahead and given my name to that Steinway dealer in Las Vegas.) When I met Don Kemp, the owner of Southern Nevada Music, and told him my name, he said, "I know about you." He gave me work right away. Don was a very talented businessman, and even though I couldn't make money right away as a musician, he made sure I could make money as a piano tuner. I had money coming in.

So I tuned pianos. It was a matter of self-preservation. At least it kept me connected to the music business. I had learned to tune pianos while at Syracuse University from a gentleman named Mr. Metzger. I never knew his first name. He was a genius at tuning and repairing, and he said the only way he would teach me to tune was for me to learn how to fix pianos as well. I went along with his self-designed teaching program. Little did I know it would come into play for many years to come. I don't know where I would be without that skill. You wouldn't believe the number of crappy pianos I have had to play on, even now. Mr. Metzger also made sure I became a member of the Piano Technicians Guild, and he got the right tools for me. He was a real Old World craftsman, and I owe him a debt of gratitude to this day.

When my three-month waiting period was over, I could at least work some casual dates, but they weren't readily appearing. There just wasn't much available to a newcomer. I had networked my butt off ever since I got to Las Vegas, and had played for a ton of people, but even casual dates went to more established musicians.

However, I did finally get a gig. My first Las Vegas gig was with guitarist Jimmy Hassel. It was at a club that no longer exists (and whose name I'll never remember). Actually, the area where it was located is now part of the McCarran Airport complex.

I wanted to make sure the job went well. I got there early, and immediately noticed two good-looking girls sitting together in a booth. But it wasn't their looks that got my attention, it was the fact that they were kissing. I was in a gay bar. "Not that there was anything wrong with that," to quote Jerry Seinfeld, but when I went to the men's room and saw what was going on in there, I decided I would just wait and go to the bathroom when I got back home. Now that was an experience. At least I finally had a paying gig in Vegas.

CHAPTER
8

My First Honest-to-Goodness Full-Time Las Vegas Gig: Playing at the Thunderbird

I continued to network, continued to jam with my friends, and continued to play for anyone who would listen. I also kept my ears open for potential work. It was getting closer to the end of the six-month union waiting period.

One day I heard that Ronnie DiFillips, the lounge pianist at the Thunderbird, was going to leave and join Gus Bivona's group. Gus was working at the Stardust and was a well-known clarinetist back then. The Stardust was a step above the Thunderbird. The lounge at the Thunderbird featured Bob Fletcher and Vicky Lano. Vicky was a gorgeous young girl who sang exceptionally well, and she and Bob were backed up by piano, guitar, and drums. I went down to the Thunderbird while they were working and told Bob I was there to audition for the piano job. That was it. There was no appointment and no formal introduction. I just went in cold. He looked at me and said, "Okay, play the next set." So I did. I eyeballed their charts and was told that since there was no bass player, I would have to play the bass part with my left hand. That was not a problem; I knew I could do it.

I played the set, and thought I had played well. In fact, everyone seemed happy with my performance. Bob told me he would call me. I waited, but he never did. The phone never rang.

So I called him one week later and said, "Hey, you were going to call me. What's going on?" He said, "Oh, you got the job." That was it. It was like it was no big deal to him. Here I was agonizing over whether I got the job or not, and this guy treats it like calling me was an intrusion on his day. Maybe it wasn't a major thing to him, but to me it was a real break. At last, I had a real full-time gig in Las Vegas.

I was on my way, sort of.

Back then the lounges paid two hundred ninety-eight dollars a week for working six days a week, six hours a night. We were able to rent a house for two hundred eighty-five dollars a month. I had money to feed my family, buy clothes, and live somewhat of a normal life. The job at the Thunderbird was actually going quite well, and the place wasn't that bad.

There was a Latin revue in the showroom called Latin Fire, written and conducted by my soon-to-be-friend George Hernandez. As people left the Latin Fire show, they had to pass the lounge where we were playing. It was designed that way to keep people in the hotel so they would gamble.

Customers liked us, the management liked us, and even though I was doing quite well comparatively, I started to get antsy. I knew the real action was down the street with the major shows, the headline acts, and the big-name performers. I was working at the Thunderbird, while the big stars were performing at Caesars, the Dunes, the Sands, or at the recently opened Hilton. I continued to network. I continued to talk to everyone who would listen. I wanted a shot at something bigger.

I had been at the Thunderbird for several months when I got a call from Pete Lulis, who was still at Caesars. He said that Steve Lawrence and Eydie Gorme were going to be appearing at Caesars Palace for two weeks, and the house band needed an additional piano player who could play electric piano and organ. Steve & Eydie's pianist at the time was Terry Trotter.

Terry is one of the finest in our business and is currently featured on the soundtrack of *Everybody Loves Raymond*. Their conductor was Nick Perito who was, and still is, one of my heroes. He is, without a doubt, one of the best conductor-arrangers in the music business and has always been a role model for me. I was hired on Pete's recommendation.

In addition to playing for Steve and Eydie, I was required to play principal piano for the opening act, the Mike Curb Congregation. They had a big hit at the time called "Joy to the World." As principal pianist for the opening act, I was heard more prominently and got a little more attention. One night Nick Perito and Terry Trotter pulled me aside and told me that they thought I wouldn't be playing second piano very much longer. They said that some main act was bound to pick me up soon. What a compliment coming from those two men.

I found out later that Nat Brandwynne, the music director at Caesars Palace who had hired me, was equally impressed with my playing. Although I didn't know it then, that was my first big break. It just wasn't going to happen right away. When the engagement finished I went back to the Thunderbird, back to Bob and Vicky, and back to where the lights weren't quite as bright. Nothing exciting. No big shows. Man, it was a letdown after working at Caesars.

So back to meeting more people, jamming with more musicians, and continuing to check in with the musicians at the union hall. It was like seeing the same movie again for the fiftieth time. I had a taste of playing for major acts, and I wanted more. It wasn't all that bad, though. At least I was working on the Strip, and getting known.

While I was at the Thunderbird I met people like Monk Montgomery (inventor of the Fender electric bass) who was playing at the Hacienda, and Red Norvo (the famous vibraphonist), who was playing at the Tropicana. I was starting to get some notoriety from playing at the Thunderbird, and Monk invited me to his home one Sunday just to jam with some of his buddies. It was a nice comfortable place, and it had room to hold a lot of people. At Monk's place I met Bob Badgley, a great bass player, and both Monk and Bob seemed to like my playing well enough. They offered to get me noticed with some of the bigger stars.

Monk invited me to play with him at the Hacienda once in a while. I also played with Red Norvo a few times. In fact, I played with anyone who would let me sit down at the piano. I learned quickly that you have to get people to notice you if you want to get ahead. Believe it or not, through all of this I still continued to tune pianos. The two hundred and ninety-eight dollars a week that I was earning at the Thunderbird was less than what I had been making back in Syracuse, and I still had bills to pay. I was a damn good tuner, and I got to tune the pianos at the Desert Inn, including the ones in the main showroom and the top floor where the high rollers were. I didn't do it just for the money. I did it to meet the casino personnel, other musicians, and just to get my name around. I knew I wasn't going to stay at the Thunderbird forever. I had my sights set higher.

CHAPTER

9

Heading Up the Strip

I think you have to have some kind of goal in life—something to reach for, something to work toward, and something to dream about. That's what makes waking up in the morning fun. It's important to know what that goal is. If you don't know what that goal is, how will you know when you've reached it?

All I knew was that I wanted to work for major entertainers. I wanted to play in the Las Vegas showrooms. By the time I got to Vegas, most of the truly great lounge acts had graduated to the main showrooms. Louie Prima and Keely Smith were a main attraction at the Sands. Shecky Greene had gone from behind the bar to the main stage at Caesars.

Playing for what was left in the lounges was not where I wanted to be. There were still a few good acts in the lounges, but I didn't want to play the same music week after week. I loved the idea of playing for a different act every week or two, which was generally the length of each main showroom engagement.

While I was at the Thunderbird in 1972, Pete Lulis left Caesars to go on the road with Paul Anka. Paul was a major headliner, and he had a number of hit records back then. He still packs people into showrooms and theaters today. Pete, however, decided that being on the road wasn't for him. I think he simply didn't like traveling. In any event, he became the house drummer at the Dunes. The conductor of the orchestra was Earl Green and the show was the Casino De Paris Revue. The pianist, Frank Leone, was leaving, so there was an opening for a pianist with the orchestra. Earl was looking for someone to replace him, and Pete recommended me. I immediately wanted the job, and I got it purely on Pete's suggestion. I remember going to Earl's house one Sunday afternoon, meeting Earl's wife and kids, and playing somewhat of an audition. He liked the way I played, and I started with the show right away. It was early 1973, and I felt I had just climbed up another rung on the ladder.

I asked Earl Green what he remembers:

Vinnie was somebody I could count on. The fellow he replaced was always taking other jobs, and I had to find substitute pianists for a lot of the shows. It started to drive me nuts. I hated firing people. I remember Jimmy Cook, a tenor sax player taking a swing at me and chasing me into the men's room when I told him he was fired. Talk about a monotonous job... I think you'd have to have a death wish to do it fourteen years in a row. This was not an easy gig. One night the Bizzaro Brothers, a bell-ringing, dumb instrument playing act from a European country that is probably no longer on the map, decided they were sick of putting up with me. On their last night they threw a plate of spaghetti on me. It went all over my white suit. I didn't laugh, but everyone else sure did. Maybe I was just a tough taskmaster. Vinnie said I was a good disciplinarian, but some of the other musicians didn't see it that way. I was very happy to have Vinnie join the orchestra.

I was making about twenty-five dollars more a week at the Dunes than when I was at the Thunderbird, but that really didn't have any bearing on my decision to take the gig. I just wanted to play in a more upscale casino. I wanted to play in the main showroom instead of the lounge. I was still doing six nights a week, two shows a night. Earl was also paying over scale. I was happy (or at least happier).

Earl was a great conductor, and I learned a lot from him. In fact, to this day, I credit much of what I learned about conducting to him. He is a fine musician and still a close friend. The only part of this new experience I wasn't excited about was playing the exact same music night after night. This show was what is known as a "production show," so there was no deviation from the charts put in front of the band. It was a full ensemble orchestra at the Dunes, playing for a show featuring an array of semi-naked female dancers.

Now, you would think that working at one of the premier casinos on the Strip, getting paid above scale, and backing a show that features beautiful women would be the epitome of a sideman's success in Las Vegas—not necessarily. First of all, I could never see the stage. The band was set up in a converted balcony box to the left of the stage, and about fifteen feet higher than the apron. Earl had his back to the stage and would have to turn around to see what was going on. If I wanted to see what was going on, I had to stand up. The percussionist, Mark Barnett, was in front of me, and the space was so tight that one of his crash cymbals hung precariously over the railing, above a table.

One night Mark hit the cymbal really hard and it flew off the stand. It fell down into the audience, and onto the middle of a table of people having dinner. Food flew all over. Drinks splashed on everyone. If someone had a camera rolling, it could have been on *America's Funniest Home Videos*. To say the folks at the table were perturbed would be putting it mildly. I'm glad we were up high where they couldn't get to us.

Occasionally, Earl would lose his baton while conducting with a lot of emphasis. It would go over the rail, hurling into the audience like a small spear. He always kept a few extras in the box, but he was lucky he never poked any eyes out. The musicians always thought it was funny. They were just looking for something to break up the monotony. But when the cymbal went over the side, we were lucky we weren't sued.

Playing the same show every night, six nights a week, starts to get a little tiring after a while. It almost becomes automatic. You occasionally forget where you are. To break up the monotony and retain our sanity, we would sometimes pull practical jokes on each other.

During the show there were several "circus acts," such as jugglers, tumblers, and magicians. The entire orchestra wasn't needed while they performed, and just the rhythm section stayed in the box and played for the act. The rest of the orchestra members would take a break.

Dave Wheeler, the bass trombone player, always kept a spray bottle of water next to his chair to lubricate the slide of his trombone. One night when he left the box while the Fercos Jugglers came on, I thought it would be funny to unscrew the top of the bottle of water, pour part of the contents into his slide, put the cap back on, and put the bottle back next to his chair. I thought he would come back to the stand, pick up his trombone, blow into it, and water would come spraying out. That would be a real hoot.

Well, Dave came back from his little break with only about eight seconds before his cue. He was the solo instrument for the first eight bars of "Music to Watch Girls By." He blew into his horn, and damn if the slide didn't come hurling out like a missile. No spray, just a flying slide. It hit the drummer in the back of his head and almost sent him over the rail into the audience. The band became hysterical. They were all wondering what the hell it was. The rhythm section never missed a beat (once the drummer recovered), and I tried to retain my composure. That was a real lesson in physics. Trombone slides should come with warning labels.

One of the funniest things I remember that happened at the Dunes was a gag we pulled on a saxophone player who was a real jokester. He always came up with different comic relief (he thought)—things just to keep us from getting bored. We thought it would be really funny to hook up an air horn underneath his chair while he was on his break. Our percussionist brought in a can of compressed air fixed to a horn, like you would see at a football game. He very carefully tied a string to the release valve and ran it underneath the chairs and over to his space, where he could control the trigger. He even tested it a couple of times to make sure it would work. It did.

The sax player came back to the box, picked up his horn, and the percussionist pulled the string. It worked all right. *Blaaaaaat!* The saxophonist jumped about four feet straight up. The only problem was the air horn wouldn't stop. There was nothing we could do to quiet it, and we couldn't muffle it either. The audience was wondering what the hell was going on. The rest of the band was wondering if we had lost our minds. Finally, the *blaaaaaat* subsided into a *bleeet-blaaat* (kind of like a bad European police siren), and finally into a *blooooop*. Then it just died. That was enough entertainment for one day. We didn't do that gag again, either.

Still, you'd think that six days a week, two shows a night, working with nearly naked girls would have to add some excitement to the job. After a while I just got sort of "anesthetized" from looking at the girls, and so did the band. It was no big deal. I would go backstage during the shows, and there would be some of the orchestra members sitting reading magazines while naked girls were walking by.

I remember one of my friends from Syracuse coming to Las Vegas shortly after he was married and coming back stage to say hello. He left his wife at the table. We were having a good time chatting when she came looking for him. She climbed up the stairs outside the box where we were, passing about ten bare-breasted young lovelies along the way. By the time she found us (with the showgirls constantly whisking by), she was a little put out. Actually not just a little. He was lucky she didn't pull him by the ear back to the table. But to me it was just another day at work.

I stayed at the Dunes for three years. It was a great run. At one point, Joe Lano, a close friend and terrific guitarist, and I got a call from Ron Andrews asking us to write and play in a lounge show that was going to open at the new Marina Hotel.

They worked it out so that Joe and I would finish the first show at the Dunes, run across the street to the Marina, play the first show there, run back across the street to the Dunes for the second show, and then run back to the Marina for the second show. Since each hotel had a different dark night, Joe and I ended up working seven nights a week. We did that for almost two years.

I liked the musicians I worked with, and I loved playing under Earl Green. But all good things come to an end. The Marina job ended before the Dunes job did. Earl was about to lose his position as bandleader at the Dunes. I went from working seven nights a week to the possibility of being out of work.

Frederick Apcar was the promoter of the show, and his ex-wife's boyfriend was arranger-conductor Jean Leccia (pronounced "Lexia"). Frederick decided he would get rid of Earl and give Leccia the job. Jean was a Frenchman, and it was a French show. Earl told him he would stay through the Christmas season if he could keep the same musicians. He really wanted to help the people who helped him for so long. He wanted me to stay, as well as Pete Lulis and the others.

At the end of 1975, Earl lost the job at the Dunes. It was unfair to Earl, who had done a wonderful job for several years. I was really pissed that I had to go to work for Leccia because of my loyalty to Earl. I liked the job there, but I still longed to play for headline acts. Nevertheless, I resigned myself to stay at the Dunes because I needed steady work. I had a family to feed.

Little did I know what was ahead.

CHAPTER
10
Caesars!

I hated to see Earl go. I didn't know what to do. Jean Leccia called me and said he didn't know what he was going to do, who he was going to keep, and spewed a lot of other useless rhetoric. It was typical of someone who just didn't have a clue what was going on.

In the meantime Al Ramsey, the contractor for Nat Brandwynne who still was the orchestra leader at Caesars Palace, called me and said their current pianist was leaving and offered me the job as house pianist. Coincidently, it was to replace the same piano player (Frank Leone) I had replaced at the Dunes. And, oddly enough, I had been offered the same job earlier, only a month or two after I had started at the Dunes with Earl Green. That first time it was because the house pianist at Caesars had passed away unexpectedly. But since Earl took a risk with me, I thought the right thing to do at the time was to see the gig at the Dunes through and not walk out on him.

Word has a way of getting around if you don't do what you say. You don't want a reputation for not keeping your word as a musician, particularly in Las Vegas. It's like placing a bet at the crap table. You don't pull your money off the board once the dice are thrown. I immediately took the job when it was offered to me the second time.

Shortly after that, Jean Leccia called me to say he had decided to keep me on at the Dunes. I told him I had taken another job, and he was livid. He was just beside himself. Actually, I felt pretty good about going down the street, since he had been stringing me along after Earl was pushed out of his position. Nat Brandwynne at Caesars had remembered me from the two weeks I did with Steve & Eydie, and he had told Al Ramsey to give me a call. I had said "no" once. I wasn't saying "no" again. I would immediately start rehearsal for the first show of the new year at Caesars. I had no idea who the star of the first show was going to be.

I remember getting into my car and going down to Caesars for the first rehearsal. I was really looking forward to playing for different shows every two weeks. What a great change it would be from doing the same show, same tunes, twice a night, six days a week. Now I was to play for great performers in two-week stints with new songs and new shows. I was looking forward to the music conductor throwing new charts on my piano and looking forward to the challenge of being able to play whatever was put in front of me. I didn't have a fear in the world. I knew I could do it. That all changed when I saw the marquee at Caesars. It simply read: "HE'S BACK!"

I instantly knew who I would be playing for. Frank Sinatra was to be the first headliner of the year at Caesars Palace. I got goose bumps. I had trouble even concentrating on finding a place to park my car. I dropped my keys on the way into the casino. I'm lucky I didn't fall going through the door.

It didn't take me long to get past the musicians, sit down at the piano, take a look at the charts, and realize I was as nervous as hell. How could I not be? The Caesars' band had done countless shows with the Chairman of the Board, but I was the new kid on the block. I had no experience working with Frank Sinatra. The other musicians were veterans. It was like coming out of basic training and going right to the front lines. You do your job right or you're dead. Playing piano for this type of show was not akin to just being part of a section of the orchestra. There was nowhere to hide. The piano would be prominently exposed. I knew this was going to be an experience.

I found out later that Nat Brandwynne had said to Sinatra when he walked in, "Hey Frank, wait'll you hear my new piano player." He had given me an enthusiastic build up that I knew nothing about. If I had known about it, I probably would have let my nerves get completely to me, let the fallboard slam on my fingers, and fallen off the piano bench. With a little luck I was able to get through the rehearsal without throwing up.

At Caesars we had a thirty-nine-piece orchestra when Frank Sinatra appeared. There was a twenty-piece string section; five saxophonists who could double on clarinet, flute, oboe, and English horn; four trumpets; four trombones; a percussionist with tympani, xylophone, bells, and all the mallet instruments; a harpist; and a full rhythm section. Man, what a great group of top musicians. It was a real gas!

Bill Miller was Sinatra's conductor, Irv Cottler played drums, Charlie Turner was his lead trumpet player, Gene Cherico was the bassist, and Al Viola played guitar. These were people I had never met before, but they were all very well known in the music industry. I had just come from the pit at the Dunes. I was still tuning pianos in my spare time, yet here I was at the top of the Strip, in the center of the entertainment world, playing for Old Blue Eyes himself. It doesn't get any better.

Here's Charlie Turner's take on the first time we played together:

> *I didn't care for Vinnie all that much in the beginning.*
> *I think the first time I met him was when we were*
> *playing for Steve & Eydie. Here I am, thinking I am*

playing big-time lead trumpet at Caesars, and here's this young kid playing organ. I thought he was playing too damn loud. I couldn't hear a damn thing. Of course, the speaker was right next to me and the other musicians turned around and looked at me like, who the hell does Charlie think he is, complaining about volume? Their ears weren't stuck in the speaker.

After that, we became pretty good friends—maybe not "hanging-out" friends, but good friends. Vinnie used to tell me I was one of the best lead trumpet players ever, but he didn't have to say that. I knew how well I played.

Bill Miller had been Frank Sinatra's piano player through the years, and kind of fell into the conducting job. Bill is a great talent and a genuinely nice person. I learned a lot from Bill just watching him conduct. He also played piano when Sinatra was singing tunes like "Angel Eyes" or "One for My Baby," when it was just Mr. S with piano accompaniment.

The first show with Sinatra was nerve-racking for me. I remember the song list started with "I've Got the World on a String," then there was "The Lady Is a Tramp," "What's New?" "Witchcraft," "Where or When," and many of the songs I played and listened to growing up. I was confident that I knew what I was doing. I wasn't confident that Sinatra knew that I knew what I was doing. I paid extreme attention to what he said to Bill Miller. I tried to pick up on any nuances and dynamics he was looking for.

Now, after the rehearsals, it was time to play the show for real. It was opening night for Frank Sinatra at Caesars. He came on stage that night without an introduction. The applause was monstrous. Finally it died down. The orchestra started to play, and Sinatra started to sing...

"I've got the world on a string…"

And I thought to myself, I do too. Now if I can just keep my nerves together and my fingers from shaking…

11

The Stars Just Kept on Coming

Caesars Palace was definitely where the major acts were. After my first two weeks playing for Frank Sinatra, other eminent performers headlined. Sinatra was signed to work there two to four times a year, two weeks each time. That left a lot of time for other stars to appear. Many of the other performers had their own pianists. When they did I would play for their opening acts.

But the headliners—man, there were some great names. Caesars had most of the truly great stars. There was Tom Jones, Diana Ross, Tony Bennett, Lena Horne, Anthony Newley, and many others. I also got to play for Andy Williams, Buddy Hackett, Steve Lawrence & Eydie Gorme, Alan King, Ann-Margret, Shirley MacLaine, and many of the opening comics who had music.

Two of the great opening acts were Wayland Flowers and his dummy, Madame, and Edgar Bergen with Charlie McCarthy. Wayland was fantastic, but Edgar Bergen was something you had to see to believe. He was a master at making the puppets come alive.

As I sat at the piano watching Edgar work, I knew I was in the presence of true greatness. I have played for other great ventriloquists such as Willy Tyler, who I think was the greatest technical ventriloquist ever. It was always said that Edgar moved his lips, but as great as the others were, their acts were no match for the reality of Mr. Bergen's puppets. He was simply the very best.

When I actually got to watch him from the piano, those puppets started to assume lives of their own. Afterward, in his case, they were lifeless dummies, but on his lap they had been living people. It was the most amazing thing I'd ever seen. I remember having such great respect for the man as an artist. Unfortunately, Mr. Bergen passed away during his last engagement at Caesars. After the second or third night of shows, he went to bed and died.

As I got better known at Caesars, some of the main acts started requesting that I play for them. The first one who specifically asked for me was Sammy Davis Jr. George Rhodes was Sammy's conductor at that time and Paul Smith was his pianist. Paul couldn't make one of the engagements, and George asked me to fill in for him. That was really cool, because Paul is an extraordinary pianist, and George could have called any one of a number of fine, well-known pianists from L.A. I had a great time playing that engagement. Sammy Davis was unique and a lot of fun.

Not too long after that, George had a problem that precluded his coming to Las Vegas, so Paul Smith took over as conductor, and once again I got the piano chair. This was a particular thrill for me as Paul was (and is) one of my idols. Paul would do some very creative things while playing, so I tried to find my own way to do similar things in the same spots. It became great fun to see if I could impress Paul with my playing. I would go home every night after the show and work out something new for the next night. Now mind you, I was no match for the great technical prowess Paul possessed—in fact, not even close.

One night Paul brought me one of his albums that he had autographed. It said how much he appreciated my chord conception, and how he loved my playing. This still stands out to me as one of the finest compliments I ever received. That reveals one of the great things about being a musician. No matter how much you admire someone whom you perceive to be far better than yourself, the other person might also see something in you that he admires. When that happens, it is very rewarding.

I was in awe of most of the performers, but a few had their quirks. Buddy Hackett seemed to feel that if the band laughed at his jokes, we were making fun of him. He couldn't believe that we found him funny night after night hearing the same routine. To me Buddy was a comic genius, and I fell over with laughter every night, as did many of the other musicians.

Sammy Davis was a doll. He was wonderful to the orchestra. He always threw a big party for the orchestra and crew closing night. He also was an expert at quick draw. (Not the Lotto or Keno game, the cowboy-western, *High Noon* type.) He had specially-made guns and holsters and would give a demonstration of his skill during the party. It was awesome.

Alan King was very funny but kept to himself most of the time. I never got to know him very well. I don't know if anybody did, at least from the orchestra side.

No one, however, compared to Frank Sinatra. He was a legend. The credentials of playing and conducting for him catapulted my career in the music business. Without his belief in me, I probably would be just another piano player. Artists like Tony Bennett, Jack Jones, Andy Williams, Robert Goulet, and so many others, would not have known me if I hadn't worked for Mr. S.

I always looked forward to those weeks when "Sinatra" was on the marquee at Caesars. It meant that every big star would show up at one time or another. One night Peter

Bogdanovich came in with his date, Cybill Shepherd. Joe Louis was often in the crowd, as was Sugar Ray Robinson. I was standing backstage one night when I was tapped on the shoulder from behind and asked by the gentleman if he could sit in a chair that I was blocking. The gentleman turned out to be Orson Welles. Gregory Peck, Kirk Douglas, Clint Eastwood, Mel Tillis, Vic Damone, Tony Curtis, and even John Wayne were frequent guests at Sinatra engagements.

Dean Martin would come in from time to time. He was truly a funny man. He could really break up Sinatra, and that was hard to do. I got to know Dean a little and found him charming. He would come into the dressing room at Caesars and have dinner with Mr. Sinatra and me. He would have us in stitches without even trying.

I never got used to being in the company of these people, but, even so, I found most of them to be warm and sincere in the conversations I had with them. I was also privileged to meet and get to know some of the greatest musicians and arrangers of our time. Don Costa, Nelson Riddle, Billy May, and Gordon Jenkins were acquaintances, if not friends.

Gordon Jenkins was especially good to me. He came to a show one night at Caesars and after the show asked Sinatra about me. Mr. S asked Gordon what he thought of my work, and Gordon gave him an excellent review. When he came out of the dressing room, I happened to be standing nearby. Gordon then introduced himself to me and asked me if I could take constructive criticism. Hell yes, I jumped at the chance. He invited me to come to his home in Malibu for some critiquing the next time I was in the L.A. area.

I took him up on the offer during my next engagement in L.A. I called and ended up spending two days with him. He gave me lessons in conducting, tips on writing, and showed me examples of how to arrange for large orchestras. We became good friends. The music world lost a tremendous talent when he passed away in 1984.

He once told me to never take my eyes off of Mr. S when I was conducting. "The orchestra needs to see your hands, but they don't need to see your face," he said. That was one of the best tips anyone ever gave me, and I've applied it to everyone I've conducted since. If you watch the singer, you can tell what's going to happen next. When I look at the person for whom I am conducting, I can see the vibrato, I can see when it's going to end, I can see the breath that's going to continue, I can see when the voice is up to par or not, and then I conduct the orchestra and make them meld with what he's doing, rather than force the singer to do what the orchestra is doing. Some of the other conductors never looked at Sinatra, and that got them in trouble.

Of course, conducting is like anything else; you have to have the perception for it. Some people could watch it for a hundred years and never understand what it really is. I was lucky. I understood what Gordon was trying to tell me, and I've used it my whole career.

CHAPTER
12
Respecting Position with Sinatra

When I started playing piano for Frank Sinatra at Caesars, there were no long conversations with him. We didn't really talk. He had his job, and I had my job. I played the very best I could, show after show, every night of the week. I studied the charts intensely and made sure I knew every note with every subtle nuance. I wanted to make sure I could play them as well as anybody. For me it was a crash course. You either did it well or you didn't do it—no talk, just action.

Mr. Sinatra was at his best every night with what seemed to be little or no effort. He was "the Chairman of the Board" and really was a show business icon. He was unique, and there will never be anyone like him. It was a long time before I got to know him, even a little bit. Just like the first night I worked for him, he always came out on stage with no introduction—every show, no intro. He always said, "I don't need an introduction. If they don't know who I am by now…" It was like Moses coming down from the mountain. People were simply in awe.

I can't say that we never spoke. We did. There was some passing conversation, a little bit here, a little bit there. But playing piano for Mr. S was not getting to know Mr. S. The first time I actually talked to him was when I knew that, after his engagement at Caesars, he was going to appear in Syracuse.

This was before I started going on the road with him. At that point I was just playing piano for him at Caesars Palace. After a rehearsal, and as he was walking off the stage, I called out, "Mr. Sinatra, could I talk to you for a second?" He turned to me and said, "Shoot!" (The same expression he often used to cue me onstage.) I said, "I know you're going to Syracuse, which is my hometown, and my parents live there, and I know you've sold out there, but I wonder if there might be some way I could get them tickets?" He said nothing. He just motioned me to wait there, and walked into his dressing room.

Within five minutes one of his people came out and said, "Are you Vinnie Falcone?" I said, "Yes," and he said, "Well, Mr. Sinatra got four tickets for you for Syracuse." That's when I knew that at least he didn't dislike me. I was told later that he went into the dressing room and immediately picked up the phone and called his office and said, "I want four tickets for Syracuse, for the kid who plays piano." How cool was that?

Thinking back, I realize that anytime I thought I was talking with him at length, it was just a few words. But after a while, the few words grew into longer sentences, and then it got to the point where we would start discussing the arrangements.

The second time Frank Sinatra returned to Caesars while I was the house pianist, I remembered that he liked the "bottom" of the orchestra. He liked big ballads, with fat lush strings, and loved the bass notes—the bass trombone, the celli, and the deep sounds. I think part of it may have been because it was easier for him to hear deep sounds as he got older and his hearing declined. The first time at Caesars he asked me to double the bottom of the orchestra with the piano—that is duplicate what the low sections of the orchestra were doing. When he was back, I did it without being told because I remembered it from the first time around. When I did it he turned to me and said, "Yeah...yeah, kid." I can't express how good that made me feel.

It was like getting an "A" in a test in school, or the teacher putting a star on your report.

During one of the Caesars Palace engagements, just prior to my starting to travel with him, they brought in a brand new arrangement that we later recorded on the album *She Shot Me Down*. It's a medley of two songs: "The Gal That Got Away" and "It Never Entered My Mind." Nelson Riddle had arranged the songs individually, and Sinatra had performed them in years past. But now he decided he wanted to make a medley of the two.

So he had Don Costa put them together, and as it worked out, "It Never Entered My Mind" ended up in the middle of "The Gal That Got Away." "It Never Entered My Mind" was arranged to be played by either the full orchestra or with solo piano accompaniment. I think this was the first test that he gave me. We were rehearsing the medley, and we got to the section where we went into "It Never Entered My Mind," and he waved the orchestra off and he pointed to me. I played it alone with him. Then we rehearsed it with the orchestra as well.

I fully expected that when I came back to do the show that night, it would be with the orchestra. But, just to be on the safe side, I went home after the rehearsal and woodshedded the accompaniment. I practiced until I knew it backward, forward, and sideways. If I was going to play this thing alone, I would know exactly how it went, and how I wanted to do it.

I didn't even think of it again until I got back there that night. The solo accompaniment had slipped my mind until Frank Sinatra's pal Jilly Rizzo came out of the dressing room and said, "Hey kid, you know that medley? Well, Frank wants you to do it. No orchestra. Just you." I played it, and Mr. S introduced me for the first time. Man, what a feeling. What a rush. My knees shook. Frank Sinatra is recognizing me. This wasn't Luigi's in Syracuse. This wasn't the Park Motor Hotel in Niagara Falls. This was the real thing.

There was another song Mr. S used to do, called "All by Myself," which had a piano solo in it, and he would mention my name. That was also a big deal for me, because Bill Miller was still his primary pianist. I was what you would call the "orchestral pianist," so when it came time for any arrangements with piano and voice alone, Bill Miller would come to the piano, and I would get up and move. But that happened less and less frequently as time went on. Sinatra kept giving me more to play.

One day in a rehearsal he brought in something that had a piano solo in it, so I got up to move for Bill, but Frank Sinatra turned to me and said, "No, you sit down and play it." That's when I started going on the road with him. And that's when I started to get into actual conversations with him. But those first conversations only involved music.

The first road trip I took with Frank Sinatra was to Harrah's in Lake Tahoe. I had always wanted to go to Harrah's because of its reputation, and here was my chance. Up to that point I hadn't been outside the Las Vegas city limits very much. This was the first great experience with Mr. S out on the road. Here we were at Harrah's in Lake Tahoe, one of the premier show places in the country at that time. Bill Harrah the owner was still alive, and he treated entertainers like kings. He also had more collector cars than anyone and, in fact, he had his own museum. I wanted to bring my wife up to Lake Tahoe to be with me and share this wonderful experience. From Las Vegas, she would have to fly to Reno and then take some sort of surface transportation up to Lake Tahoe. It took about an hour to make the trip.

Since I had no car with me, I decided that, before renting a car to pick up my wife, I would ask the hotel if there was some sort of shuttle service I could use for the trip to Reno and back. They must have relayed my request to Mr. Harrah, because I received a call from the transportation desk informing me that I would be chauffeured to and from Reno when my wife's plane arrived. Not only was I chauffeured but they also took me in one of Mr. Harrah's classic Rolls Royce Touring Sedans. My wife almost fainted when she saw the car.

During the Lake Tahoe engagement, Mr. S began to introduce me as one of his guys. What a kick. After that trip, nothing was said to me about whether I was in or out, or even whether I was going or staying. I just started getting plane tickets and trip sheets from the office. I was never officially hired. Hell, I didn't need an official proclamation. I said nothing; I was just happy to be chosen.

CHAPTER

13

Playing Piano Was One Thing, Conducting Was Something Else

It was spring of 1977, and I was traveling with Sinatra quite a bit. At this time Jilly Rizzo was representing a beautiful young singer named Marlene Ricci. He was successful in getting her to open the show. She also was the star of a TV show about Caesars Palace entitled *Cinderella at the Palace*.

One night on the road, her conductor was held up by a delayed flight. They asked me to conduct for her. Mr. Sinatra watched me, and I think it was then that he decided to replace Bill Miller with me. Soon after he called for me to come down to his house in Palm Springs, California. When Jilly picked me up at the airport, he asked me if anyone had talked to me yet. I said, "About what?" He immediately clammed up. I had no idea what was going on.

While I was in Palm Springs, Mr. Sinatra took me to his piano, and started teaching me his vocal exercise routine without telling me why. He had begun preparing me. One evening Barbara Sinatra said to me that either way I was "in." I hadn't the faintest idea what she meant. (She told me later that they had been considering making me either Marlene's conductor or giving me a shot at being Sinatra's conductor).

Mr. Sinatra devised somewhat of a scheme. He had Don Costa call me and tell me that they, Sinatra and Costa, were going into the studio to record three songs, and that Mr. S wanted me to conduct the orchestra. I asked if Bill Miller would be there, and I was told that he wouldn't. I couldn't believe it! I flew to Burbank, California, where Costa picked me up and took me to Warner Brothers Studio in Burbank.

When I arrived, Mr. Sinatra was in a room with his secretary going over his mail. He greeted me, but said nothing more. He then instructed Don to take me into the studio and introduce me to the orchestra. These were the top studio musicians who played for many of the movie soundtracks in Hollywood. I recognized some of the best musicians in the world in that orchestra, and I was going to conduct them.

The air conditioning failed that night, and I was so nervous that I was perspiring on the music and actually blotting sweat off the notes. We did three songs, after which Sinatra said nothing to me. Don Costa took me back to the airport, and I flew home. My wife asked me what was up. I told her that I really had no idea, but that it had been one of the most exciting nights of my life.

Nothing further was said to me, and at our next engagement (which was in Reno), Bill Miller was back and everything returned to normal. At least that's what I thought. Sinatra told me later that he held the recording session just to see how I would do. Apparently I passed the test. It was all leading up to a real turning point in my career.

I was at home in the kitchen with my wife when I got a phone call. It was Mr. Sinatra's manager. We were supposed to go to Radio City Music Hall in New York City, and, of course, I was planning to go as the pianist. I guess he chose that engagement to see if I could handle the conductor spot. He was testing me. He believed in trial by fire, so there was no breaking me in slowly. He wanted to start me as conductor at Radio City Music Hall, with every dignitary and famous New York musician in the audience. That was the kind of confidence he had, not only in me, but also in himself.

His manager called me up and said, "Hey Vinnie, Frank wants you to conduct, can you handle it?" I thought for a couple of seconds. What am I going to say? No? I knew I had only two choices. If I said no, I would never get another chance. If I said yes, I would either make it or fail. Failing wasn't an option for me, so I said, "Yes, of course, yes!"

I had confidence in myself. But I didn't know how I was going to be received, and I didn't know what the chemistry with the musicians was going to be. I think Mr. Sinatra perceived that before I did. When I went to New York, I met considerable resistance from a lot of people. Resistance wasn't even the right word. Jealousy was more like it. Here's this young man, less experienced than anybody else, and he's going to be the leader? There were a lot of eyes rolling.

I went to the first rehearsal with the orchestra at NBC in Rockefeller Plaza. That orchestra was comprised of the finest musicians in New York City—or anyplace else for that matter. I was looking at many of my heroes sitting in the orchestra. Countless recordings that I had listened to as a kid featured many of these great players. The concertmaster was Joe Malin, who, along with his wife, Carmel, became personal friends. Joe and many of the other members of this spectacular orchestra sort of took me under their wings and helped me "make it through the night," so to speak. They saw to it that I had the advantage of their years of experience, and they gave it to me without reservation.

After the first rehearsal, Mickey Rudin (Mr. Sinatra's manager) asked Joe how I had done. Joe said, "The kid's going to be fine." I didn't know this until years later, but things like that helped me gain the confidence of the people around Mr. Sinatra. I found out much later, from the man himself, that he had little doubt that I would do well. He had more confidence in me than I had in myself. When I would do something wrong, or something that I could have done better, one of the orchestra members would quietly pull me aside and straighten me out. I listened to every word that the orchestra members said to me.

Without these great people, I would not have made it. Sinatra was not one to take time explaining what he wanted. He expected you to pay close attention and figure it out for yourself. I realized that early on, and I made every effort to anticipate his musical needs. I believe that, more than anything else, this realization kept me in his good graces. In all the years I was with him, he never once raised his voice to me nor did he tell me how to conduct or play. He knew that I had my radar on at all times, and that I would always pay close attention to what he was doing musically.

I have little recollection of opening night at Radio City. I remember Sinatra saying to me, "Let's go, Vinnie," just before we went on stage. I was so nervous. Man, you can imagine... Radio City Music Hall! To me, it would have made more sense to break me in at a place like Toledo, Ohio, or Lincoln, Nebraska, but not New York, New York. I remember walking on stage that night and the one thought that went through my mind as I was walking behind him was, "Holy Christ! This is not a rehearsal anymore; I can't make a mistake." My concentration level was so severe that the next thing I can remember is walking back to the hotel wondering if I had done well enough to please him.

I think it was the third night when I went in to warm up with him that he paused, looked at me and said, "This is going to be quite marvelous." (Actually he pronounced it "*mahvelous.*") It was a word he liked to use a lot. And when he said that to me, I didn't understand the significance of it to the degree I came to understand later through working and spending more time with him. But that was his way of telling me that I had passed the test. I indeed was "in." Barbara was right. Looking back, I realize that Radio City was only the beginning of an interesting part of my musical career.

CHAPTER
14
I Never Called Him Frank

Frank Sinatra was big on respect. To get it, you had to give it. It was difficult to get to know the Chairman of the Board. It was even more difficult to be in his inner circle. One thing was for sure: If you *wanted* "in," you were "out." I learned to keep my distance when I had to. Italians are big on respect. I had learned that from my family, and it paid big dividends playing for Sinatra.

My relationship with Mr. Sinatra was very much a teacher-student, father-son mentoring relationship. It never became Frank and Vinnie, it was always Mr. Sinatra and Vinnie. I called him Mr. S or Boss. I never ever called him Frank, yet he was the one who gave me the nickname Vinnie. However, during a performance he always made a point of using my full name. When he introduced me to the audience I was always Vincent Falcone.

He was the "old man" to most of the musicians in the band. I was only around him when he wanted me to be. I never tried to insert myself, which I found to be the secret of getting along with him. And the more I observed that philosophy, the more I was around him.

Often I traveled with him. Of course that raised the ire of many people that had been with him a lot longer than I had. In fact, it pissed off a lot of the people who had been there before me, but that's the way it was. We became, in my estimation, not only friends, but we could and did tell each other things that would normally be discussed only between close friends. For me it was a cherished relationship. But it was always with respect for a man who was old enough to be my father.

Only after conducting at Radio City Music Hall did Mr. Sinatra and I really start discussing anything. First we talked about musical things and then, as we spent more time together, we started talking about family. As I grew to know him better, he began to talk about personal things and he started to open up to me a little more. It was interesting to hear him reflect. He would tell me tales about the old days, the glory days of Las Vegas.

He also told me very moving stories about his family and funny stories about the people he met over the years. Every once in a while he would tell me stories about when he worked for the "boys," because they used to own all the clubs. He was often accused of knowing the mob. He told me that in his early years of performing it was impossible to be in show business and not know some of the mob because, for the most part, they controlled the nightclubs. But he certainly did not want to be identified with the mob.

It was wonderful to hear the stories of his youth and also about his amazement with the fanatical treatment he received from the public. I think, however, that he learned to deal with it very quickly. He knew who he was. I saw world leaders grovel at his feet. It was amazing. His stories were all so interesting because they were about famous people, and included some of the most important and influential people on earth.

He told me about his mother. He had great respect for her. He said she had been involved with local politics, and was very powerful and respected in her community.

As he talked to me about his mother, I recalled the night she died. Sinatra was performing Caesars Palace and I was still house pianist at the time. His mother was flying in from Palm Springs for the show. I was not yet close to Sinatra and I didn't know she hadn't yet arrived when the show began.

He went on and did the first show. When I came back to do the second show there was a pall backstage that you could cut with a knife. I asked what was going on and they told me she was missing and that there had been no report of an accident. He went ahead and did the second show, but when he sang "My Funny Valentine," he actually broke down crying.

During the course of the evening it was revealed that the plane had been lost and he cancelled the rest of the engagement. Two days later they found the plane buried in the snow on the top of a mountain. The weather had been bad the night that the plane had disappeared. Apparently the pilot had become disoriented and hit the mountaintop.

Sinatra also told me of his father and the love he had for him. He believed that there would one day be a movie made about his life, and he told me that he wanted Martin Balsam to play his dad, and Robert DeNiro to play him.

He talked a great deal about his days with Tommy Dorsey. He related to me his utmost respect for Tommy as a player, but most of all for the way he handled being a leader. When describing to me the best way to handle certain situations pertinent to the orchestra, he would always refer to the way Tommy would handle it. I believe that Sinatra's mother and Tommy Dorsey were the two biggest influences in his life. I liked hearing about the old days, and the musicians from the past. Sinatra talked about the old days, the mob, the women, the music, and I listened.

As I understand, he grew up in the school of hard knocks. He learned by keeping his eyes open and his mouth shut. He learned from Tommy Dorsey and all those people, but nobody ever came to him and said: If you do it like this, you're going to be a success. Frank Sinatra was the innovator, and he was the one who decided when he should go out on his own, and he was the master of his destiny. He expected this of everyone else. He would never tell me if I was doing something wrong. It was up to me to figure it out. If I didn't figure it out, I just wasn't going to be there next week.

We never talked much about the women he had had in his life, but I remember him commenting one time, "If I had been with as many women as the press liked to talk about, I would have been put in a jar at Harvard Medical School."

When Mr. S was in a reflective mood, he liked to talk about when he was young and how things came together for him. He told me about growing up on the streets of Hoboken, New Jersey. You've read about them in other books. I was getting them firsthand.

It was easier talking to him about today than the early years. I was glad I came after Ava Gardner, after the Rat Pack, after Sam Giancana, and after President Kennedy. This was a softer side of Frank Sinatra. It was a side of Sinatra a lot of people didn't know existed. Make no mistake, however, he knew what he wanted, and made sure he got it. His favorite expression to those who didn't shape up was, "Where you workin' next week?"

I remember Mr. S telling me about the days with Harry James. I think he really liked Harry. One night at a performance at the Universal Amphitheater, Harry came to see the show. He was in the dressing room with us before the show, and Sinatra invited him to get his horn and do a number with us. Harry looked at me and said to Sinatra, "Can the kid play?" The old man told him not to worry and Harry played a couple of songs with us. As you can imagine, with the two of them together the audience went wild.

After a while, Mr. Sinatra loosened up with me to the point where we shared a lot of laughs. He had a great sense of humor. He also had a heart of gold.

When I was with him, he always included me, no matter who else was in on the conversation. He once introduced me to Pete Fountain as his "leader." He would take me with him to dinner after the show to places like 21 in New York, and when we were abroad, we went to the best restaurants.

He loved my wife, Connie, and treated her like a queen. I particularly remember one night at a party in London attended by Ingrid Bergman, Claudette Colbert (whom he called Frenchy), and many other dignitaries and movie stars. My wife asked to be excused to go to the ladies room, and to her amazement, he sent his security guard with her for protection. She never got over that.

I saw him help so many people who could not help themselves. I know that he sent Joe Louis to Dr. DeBakey after Joe had a stroke. He was generous with people he didn't know. He once received a letter from a woman who told him that for all her life she had wanted to see him in person, but never had the chance. Now we were going to appear somewhere near to where she lived, but she was now an invalid and couldn't get to the arena. He instructed Dorothy, his secretary, to send a limo for the woman, give her a prime seat, and then take her home. No one knew of these acts of kindness unless you happened to be privy to them. I was witness to countless generous acts that never became public knowledge.

One of his favorite expressions was, "Duke 'em a C note." He would say that when he wanted one of his aides or body-guards to give somebody a hundred dollar bill as a tip. It could be a waiter, a bellhop, or just somebody going out of his way for him. One day he was waiting for his car outside a casino, and when the car pulled up, he asked the young parking attendant what the biggest tip he ever received was. The attendant told him a hundred dollars. Sinatra gave him two hundred dollars, and then asked who had given him the hundred-dollar tip. The kid replied, "You did, sir, last week."

He was also a dichotomy. Once we were in London, leaving Albert Hall after an afternoon rehearsal. He and I were riding together, and as we exited the hall via a back door, a man took his picture without asking permission. Mr. S had his bodyguard confiscate the man's camera and remove the film. He gave the man one-hundred-dollar compensation for the film. At exactly that moment, a woman on the other side of the street called out to him in a cockney accent and said, "Hey Frankie, can I have a photo?" He called back to her and said, "Take as many as you want, baby," and stood quietly while she took several photos. You see, she asked.

He was very loyal to those who had been around him for a long time. When the Shah of Iran was in a hospital in New York after having been overthrown, Mr. S went to see him regardless of what anyone thought.

He always helped those who had helped him in the past. Once we were on our way to Atlantic City from New York, and when we got to Hoboken, New Jersey, where he was born, he had the driver take a detour to an old house in town. He told me to wait in the car while he went inside. After a few minutes, he called down to me from a second-story porch. With him was a very old man. They waved to me and I yelled up a "hello" to the old man. When he returned to the car, he told me that the man upstairs had given him his first job at a Hoboken newspaper when he was a kid. He never forgot that man, and made it a point to stop and see him from time to time.

Another time when we were in Atlantic City performing at Resorts International, Sinatra gave me the names of four men who lived in the vicinity. It turned out that they were the musicians who had worked with him when he got his start at the Rustic Cabin. He instructed me to find them and invite them to a dinner that he hosted in their honor. Burt Lancaster came along too. Burt happened to be in town filming the movie

Atlantic City. They all came and had a great evening of swapping stories about the "old days."

I didn't know Mr. Sinatra before he came back from retirement. I'm glad I was there during his "second tour of duty." He was truly a singer's singer, an American legend, and just one unique, great individual.

CHAPTER

15

Nice 'n Easy
(Most of the Time)

When I started with Mr. Sinatra, I got paid more than the two hundred ninety-eight dollars per week I made as a house pianist at Caesars. He guaranteed me thirty-five thousand dollars a year (a lot of money back then) and let me play other gigs when he wasn't using me. I had stuck to my goal and I was finally achieving the success I had hoped for. I think in order to be a successful musician today, for those who are not headliners, you have to kind of roll with the punches and take the good with the bad. Being able to adapt is key. I liked going out on the road with Frank Sinatra, but it was not all private jets and limos. We traveled by plane most of the time and stayed in some pretty ordinary hotels.

You would think that having the job as pianist-conductor for the Chairman of the Board would have plenty of perks and benefits. It did. But not everything was as pleasant as you might imagine.

The first musicians I worked with after becoming the conductor were the New York City musicians from the AFM Local 802. These men and women were among the finest musicians in the world, bar none. They accepted me with open arms, and they helped me get through my learning curve without going over too many bumps. They became close friends over the years. Thank God for their help, because I didn't get much guidance from the Sinatra guys. I made it a point to show them respect since they were there before me, but sometimes it was a real lesson in futility.

For instance, the first time I met Mickey Rudin, who was Sinatra's manager, I held out my hand to him and said what a pleasure it was to meet him. He ignored my hand and said, "I don't shake hands with musicians." Charlie Turner, lead trumpet, was not easy to get along with at the start, but he came around after a short while, and we still remain friends. The guitarist, Al Viola, and the bassist, Gene Cherico, were not hostile to me, but they were of little or no help.

The real problem was the drummer, Irv Cottler. Irv had been with Mr. Sinatra for many years, and he considered himself to be the real leader of the group. I tried in every way to develop a strong relationship with him, and he made me believe he was in my corner. However, I found out later that he was working against me from the start. I never fully understood why he was so difficult.

Every time Mr. Sinatra would show me any attention, preference, or take me with him on his private plane, Irv would become incensed. It would drive him nuts. He always accused me of trying to have him replaced as the drummer. I told him so many times that I respected his position, his talent, and that, even if I wanted to replace him, I wouldn't do it out of respect.

After five years with Sinatra, I asked Irv if he realized that if I could replace him, I would have already fired him by then. My only consolation was that he had done similar things to Don Costa and Nelson Riddle when they were conducting. They both told me stories of several instances when they had had similar problems with Irv. Irv seemed to fear *any* musician to whom Sinatra paid attention. That was a shame because I know that Sinatra loved Irv's playing and would never have let him go.

Charlie Turner, lead trumpet player, remembers:

I played with Sinatra for about ten years. The only one who played longer than I was Irv Cottler the drummer, and he was a pain in the ass. He was jealous and could drive you crazy. He wanted to lead the orchestra. Any time another musician got too close to Frank, he wanted to torpedo the relationship. I was good friends with Irv in the beginning, but then we went to Europe, and I started getting a few more solos and Irv started getting upset. One time he threw one of his drums across the stage. One thing I have to say about Vinnie though, he never got into pissing contests with Irv. He just took it and let it go. I think the most upset I heard him get was when he told Cottler, "Kiss my ass." There were many times when I think Vinnie should have just decked him.

I tried many times to make peace with Irv. Without my knowledge, Irv was telling Mickey Rudin that I was not doing my job well, and that I did not have the respect of the orchestras with which we were performing. Mr. Rudin tended to believe Irv's rants, and once called me into his office and told me that the only reason I was still in the job was that I made Frank Sinatra happy.

I got my due on one engagement in London. The orchestra gave a party for Sinatra to thank him for all the years he had been coming to England and performing with them. During the party, the concertmaster toasted Mr. Sinatra and then said how much they enjoyed my conducting and piano playing. I was standing next to Sinatra when this was said. Irv turned and walked out of the room. It was awful, just awful. I felt absolutely terrible.

Thinking back, I never saw or talked to Irv after 1986. He passed away a few years later, and I heard that he died alone. I was sorry we were never friends.

Al Viola is a lovely man and a fine guitarist. Although we never hung out much together, there were times when he was quite charming and very humorous. I remember once when I helped him carry some of his baggage to his room in a hotel where we were staying. He asked the bellman to bring him a "board." Both the bellman and I interpreted it to mean a board to put between the mattress and the box spring to make the bed firmer. Al did not let on to me that this was one of his pranks. When the bellman returned with the board, Al said to him "No, no, no, I said bring me a BROAD!" I know that Al loved Sinatra, and it was brought home to me just how much when, at Sinatra's funeral, he broke down and cried as we greeted each other.

Gene Cherico was always a mystery to me. He had a fine reputation as a bassist, but I had some problems with him. He would get lost in the music quite often, even though he had been playing it for years. It was like he didn't know where he was mentally. It would always seem to happen just when I needed him the most. He had a very good "time feel," and that was what Mr. Sinatra liked about him. It was Gene who first made me aware of the severity of the problem I was having with Irv.

In my opinion, Charlie Turner was, if not the best, one of the best lead trumpet players ever. When I gave the downbeat, Charlie was *always* right there. Charlie, Larry "Nifty" Victorson (Sinatra's personal assistant), and I always had great laughs together. Charlie lives in Florida now, and he, along with Bill Miller and myself, are the last living musicians of the Sinatra clan.

I will always love Bill Miller for the chance that he gave me, and I will always admire his ability as an accompanist. I learned a great deal from him, and I think his rendition of "One for My Baby" is the definitive version. When I play it, I am always influenced by his treatment.

The last of Mr. Sinatra's personal musicians during my tenure was Tony Mottola. Tony replaced Al Viola. Tony was one of the sweetest men who's ever lived, as well as one of the finest guitarists in our business. He and his wife, Mitzi, were so very good to my wife, Connie, and me—both socially and, in Tony's case, musically. Tony added a whole new dimension to the guitar chair. Mr. S would feature Tony in the show much the way he featured me, by letting Tony solo and perform solo numbers with Sinatra. Tony had recorded many solo albums in his career, and Sinatra recognized the value of having such a well-known musician on his staff. Tony remained my friend and mentor until his death in 2004.

At first, Jilly Rizzo didn't seem to be fond of me either. Jilly was a unique man, and Sinatra would refer to Jilly as the brother he never had. At one time he and Sinatra had a falling out. I couldn't believe it because Jilly had been so close to him. He was a real Damon Runyon character. We became better friends as the years passed.

Dorothy Uhleman was Mr. Sinatra's secretary. A harder-working woman has never lived. She did everything for him, as well as satisfy all his fans who needed attention. You can imagine the influx of mail she would have to go through every day. I had great affection for her. She and her husband, Ernie, were always very nice to me. It was certainly much appreciated, particularly when things weren't going smoothly.

I think if you want to make it today as a musician, you also have to have role models. You need people to coach you, to give you advice, and to help you through the times when a four-lane highway turns into a dirt road. One of the people who made my life easier was Sid Cooper, who was the lead saxophonist with the New York orchestra. He was, however, much more than that.

His career includes playing with Tommy Dorsey, The Tonight Show Orchestra, plus a ton of other musical main events. He is an accomplished arranger and can be heard on many recordings. I could always count on Sid to help me through any musical problems I encountered.

Other people who helped me were Teddy Sommer, a terrific percussionist and drummer for Rita Moreno, as well as Joe Malin, the orchestra contractor and concertmaster, and his wife, Carmel. They were as close to me as anyone can get. Joe is gone, but Carmel still runs the business and provides orchestras for me, and others, when we perform in the New York area.

During my years with Sinatra, I came to know Nelson Riddle, Don Costa, Gordon Jenkins, and Billy Byers. These are four of the greatest American arrangers of all time. You can imagine what I learned from these great men. I was in awe of them, but I made sure I absorbed whatever they told me. In the case of Billy Byers, I got to work with him outside of the Sinatra circle. He was an extraordinary arranger by virtue of his ability to handle so many different styles—from jazz to Broadway and everything in between.

One thing I learned from working with such an array of musicians and cast of characters was this: You can't always be friends with everyone, and not everyone will like you. You do the best you can with whomever you have to work. If you're not getting along with somebody, it is not your problem; it is their problem. You have two choices in life when things aren't going easily: you can accept it the way it is, or you can do something about it. I decided early in my career no one was going to make things so hard for me that I couldn't overcome it. Life is too short.

16

Recording *Trilogy* and "New York, New York"

I had been in the job of conductor for about two years when I learned we were going to return to Warner Brothers Studios in Burbank to record. Once again we had a fantastic orchestra. By now I was much more self-confident, but the presence of Victor Feldman playing percussion, Dick Nash and George Roberts playing trombone—not to mention concertmaster Jerry Vinci, and so many other notable musicians in this session—not only made me a bit nervous, it also kept me on my toes.

We were into about our third song when Sonny Burke, one of the most prominent and respected record producers in the business, entered the studio and began talking with Sinatra. He and Mr. Sinatra got into a very long and animated discussion that I was not privy to at first. After some time Mr. Sinatra came back to the main studio and dismissed the orchestra for the night. He then gathered Don Costa, Sonny Burke, and myself together. He told us that Sonny had a great idea for a new recording and that we were going to put everything on hold until Sonny had put it all together. He vowed that we would not record another note until this project was ready to go.

The project was *Trilogy*. Sonny's idea was to have three records packaged into one jacket; each one of the three records would represent a period of Sinatra's musical life. They would be called *The Past*, *The Present*, and *The Future*. Sinatra wanted Nelson Riddle to do *The Past*, Don Costa to do *The Present*, and Gordon Jenkins to do *The Future*.

I was in the dressing room in the suite at Caesars Palace with Sinatra, shouting Nelson Riddle's praises, when Sinatra turned to me and said, "Call Nelson on the phone and ask him if he will write a chart for me." And I thought, "Wow, man, I'm going to be a part of history here." I was a casual friend of Nelson's, so I picked up the phone and called him: "Nelson, Mr. Sinatra asked me to call you. He would like to know if you would write an arrangement..." And there was dead silence on the other end of the phone for a good ten or fifteen seconds and then Nelson said, "Tell him I'm busy." And he hung up. I told Sinatra, and he said, "Who needs him?" Actually, it was something stronger, but you get the picture.

Nelson Riddle and Sinatra had had a falling out some years earlier. The disagreement had been over a testimonial dinner for Riddle that Sinatra was supposed to attend. Sinatra had to cancel because his business manager had him booked on that date, so they rescheduled the dinner. It was an incredible feat to reschedule with all the celebrities that would be in attendance, but they did it. They sold out the house at a thousand dollars a plate, and Mr. S cancelled again because of a booking. I don't know why Sinatra didn't overrule it. I mean, who can imagine a tribute to Nelson Riddle without Frank Sinatra? I never discussed it with Mr. S. It was a touchy subject.

In the end, they got Billy May to do *The Past*.

Everyone went to work on this project. Billy stuck to those songs that Sinatra had recorded in his early years, together with a few songs that he had liked but had not recorded. Don Costa wanted to take the best songs from 1960s and '70s and treat them in the Sinatra style. Gordon Jenkins had the hardest task.

He was to write original material that would musically describe Sinatra's future.

Since Mr. Sinatra knew most of the songs that were to be on *The Past* and *The Present*, the real challenge was to learn all the original music being composed by Gordon Jenkins. However, there were also a couple of tunes from *The Present* that were unfamiliar to Sinatra. Among them were "You and Me" by Peter Allen and Carol Bayer Sager and "Just the Way You Are" by Billy Joel. Costa wrote an unbelievable chart for "You and Me," but when he got to "Just the Way You Are," he treated it in much the same style as Billy Joel had. I really didn't think it worked. I had this idea in the back of my mind for a treatment of "Just the Way You Are." We were working at Caesars Palace at the time, so I spent a few days at home working it out.

When I had the treatment the way I wanted it, I asked Sinatra if I could play it for him. After I finished playing it for him, he said, "Call Don and tell him that's what I want." From his suite, I called Don and played it for him over the phone. He was a bit ticked off with me at first because he had already completed about fifty percent of the arrangement his way. He started over and created one of the most swinging charts on the album. When Billy Joel heard it, he called Sinatra to tell him how much he liked it.

It is a never-ending source of pride for me that I had a role, however small, in the development of the *Trilogy* project. What a great recording! When finally released in 1980, *Trilogy* went gold in a matter of weeks. It truly summed up Frank Sinatra's career. You still see it stocked in record stores and it continues to sell long after it was made.

We spent the better part of a year in preparation for *Trilogy*. I was with Mr. S almost continually, helping him learn the original material that was *The Future*. In between engagements, we worked at his house in Beverly Hills. When we were ready, we began in New York with Billy May. Billy's work was brilliant. If I remember correctly, we finished the entire first album in three days.

The second album was great fun. Working with Don Costa was always fun for me because Don never wanted to conduct his own charts. He always let me do it, and he stayed in the control room with the engineers. Sinatra always sang live to the orchestra, which is hardly ever done, especially today. Even when it is done, there are damn few singers who can do it. One of my all-time favorite Costa arrangements is on this album. I think Michel LeGrand, Alan Bergman, and Marilyn Bergman's "Summer Me, Winter Me" is one of the most beautiful orchestrations ever written. Also featured on *The Present* was "New York, New York," which was actually recorded twice. We did it once in New York and again in L.A.

The story of "New York, New York" is quite interesting. John Kander and Fred Ebb wrote the song for the movie of the same name starring Liza Minnelli and Robert DeNiro. Liza had recorded it and had quite a bit of success with it. One day at a rehearsal in New York Sinatra brought the sheet music and gave it to me and told me to play it for him. After hearing me play it, he decided then and there that he had to sing this song. He foresaw what he could do for this song and what the song could do for him. He had Don Costa write a new overture for the New York engagements that would contain only songs about New York and would end with the song "New York, New York." During the familiar vamp at the beginning of the song, Sinatra walked on stage and sang it as his opening selection.

The response was incredible. After a short time Sinatra decided that "New York, New York" was too strong to be an opening song and that we should move it further down in the lineup. I was instructed to remove it from the overture, which I did by writing a new ending, and then having "New York, New

York" recopied as a separate piece of music. With this accomplished, he began to move it down the lineup.

It wasn't very long before it replaced "My Way" as the closing number in his show. He also fine-tuned the phrasing and delivery of the song as he went along until it became the monster hit that it was on *Trilogy*. He was still in the process of developing it when he recorded it the first time. We kept on performing it, night after night, and he continued to make it more exciting.

Sinatra could be counted on to bring the house down with it at every show, particularly those in the New York City area. It exemplified the anger and the hostility, the ambition and the optimism, and the energy and excitement that is New York, and that was also Sinatra. By the time he reached the last chorus and the modulation of "these little town blues," the excitement of the crowd was impossible to contain.

After performing it onstage many times, Sinatra had molded it into the classic it has become. He decided to re-record it before releasing the record so he could put the more refined version on the finished album. That's the kind of dedication he had to the music.

Whenever I go to Yankee Stadium for a ball game, I always hear myself at the end of each game when they play the hit. "New York, New York" also allowed Mr. Sinatra to retire "My Way" for a time, as he had become weary of it. For a long time, he would only sing "My Way" and "Strangers in the Night" when we were abroad.

We recorded *The Future* in Los Angeles at the Shrine Auditorium. The Shrine was chosen for the acoustics. Gordon used a huge symphonic orchestra, and the sound was remarkable. I always felt badly for Gordon because the so-called "critics" who reviewed the project were unkind to him. In their ignorance, they failed to see the genius of what he had accomplished. Words, music, the entire concept: all came from one man. I thought it was brilliant. The negative reviews hurt Gordon deeply. That's when I understood what Sinatra meant when he once told me, "If critics weren't critics, they'd be snipers."

Trilogy was a huge commercial success, as well it should have been. I'm proud to have been a part of it. On the last day of recording, as we were leaving the studio, Sinatra stopped me, extended his hand, and said, "Thanks, kid." What more could I have wanted?

The last album I did with Sinatra was entitled *She Shot Me Down*. It was not a commercial success. I don't think you're going to find it in a record store or on Amazon, but there was some wonderful material on the record. Mr. S told me he wanted to give Gordon Jenkins one last project. Gordon was ill and Sinatra suspected he didn't have a lot of time left. Gordon did all the arrangements except one. That one was "The Gal That Got Away/It Never Entered My Mind." Gordon gave me the baton when we got to that song, and I both conducted it and played the piano solo. Once again I was rewarded. In his own wonderful sweet way, Gordon put his arm around me and complimented me on my work that night. That's like having Joe DiMaggio compliment you on your hitting.

It was really an era to be remembered. I am glad I was included in that moment in time. There doesn't seem to be very many Gordons, Dons, and Billys around these days.

CHAPTER
17

Swingin' with the Count

As far as I'm concerned, the greatest big band of all time was the Count Basie Orchestra. Woody Herman's band was a close second. When Sinatra told me that we were going to New York to appear with the Basie band, I was ecstatic. To meet Count Basie had always been a dream of mine, but to actually play with his band, that was more than a dream come true!

We were appearing in Las Vegas a short time before heading to New York. Sinatra was filling in for a sick Liza Minnelli at the Riviera Hotel. I was thinking about how I was going to handle standing in front of the great Basie band—and giving instructions to men who had been around forever and had been answering only to the Count.

One night before the show, Mr. S and I were in the dressing room, getting ready to go on, and I said to him, "Boss, I need your counsel. I'm not sure how to handle myself with the Basie band. On the one hand, I have to make sure they play the music the way I know you want it played, but on the other hand, I have to do it in a respectful manner. After all, they are the Count Basie Orchestra. Could you give me the benefit of your advice?" Sinatra just sat there in front of the mirror continuing to get ready. He said nothing for at least two or three minutes, then looked at me in the mirror and said, "You'll figure it out."

Another lesson from the "Man." If you can't stand the heat, get the hell out of the kitchen. Sinatra had come up the ladder by being independent and making his own decisions. He expected others to do the same. That, in my opinion, is how you earned his respect.

When we went to New York for the Basie engagement, I was told we were going to rehearse again at the NBC Studios in Rockefeller Center. I arrived early to get myself prepared. We were in a studio adjacent to where *Saturday Night Live* was broadcast. John Belushi suddenly appeared and started asking me questions about music and conducting. We had a nice talk, and then he returned to his studio to continue rehearsing the show. Before he left, he invited me to come over to his studio and watch a little of their rehearsal, and I did on one of my breaks.

By the time I returned, the Count Basie Band was starting to arrive. I didn't know any of them personally, but I did know many of them by reputation. No one talked to me. When it was time to start the rehearsal, I introduced myself to the band and told them what a pleasure it was for me to work with them. We started the rehearsal, and I soon found out that when we played the great swing charts of Sinatra, like "Pennies from Heaven," "Lady Is a Tramp," "All of Me," and "I've Got the World on a String," they were wonderful. However, when it came to the tender ballads and rubato sections of the music like "Someone to Watch Over Me," "Wee Small Hours of the Morning," and "My Shining Hour," they were not as proficient. Now I had my work cut out for me. I have to say that most of them gave me all they had, and in the end it was a wonderful experience for me. I had to work them very hard, but I always let them know how deeply I respected their musicianship.

In the middle of rehearsing one of the songs, I noticed that Count Basie had come into the room and was sitting in a chair watching me. As soon as we took our next break, I approached the Count and said to him, "Mr. Basie, I want you to know what a great honor it is to meet you and conduct your great band." He was wearing his trademark captain's cap and had a twinkle in his eye. He looked up at me and said, "I heard about your ass." He then told me to call him Bill and I told him that I couldn't do that. I had too much respect for him to call him by his first name. From then on, I called him "Pops" instead.

Mr. Sinatra had us all wear white tie and tails for the whole engagement. Can you just imagine the Count Basie band in tails? There were two nine-foot Steinway concert grand pianos facing each other in front of the band, one for me and one for the Count. Sinatra wanted Basie on stage for the entire concert. I conducted and played at one piano, while the Count sat and played at the other. At one point during the concert, just before starting the next song, Basie called to me and said, "Vinnie, what's the tempo?" I thought to myself: I must have died and gone to heaven—Count Basie's asking me what's the right tempo for a song.

I saw the Count many times after that engagement. He always remembered my name. I got to work with the Basie band again when I was with Tony Bennett in the '90s. The Count was no longer with us—he passed away in 1984—but being with his band and Tony Bennett made it special for me.

The song had ended, but the melody lingered on.

CHAPTER
18
The Reagan Inaugural Celebration

In late 1980, Mr. Sinatra told me that he had been asked to produce President-elect Reagan's inaugural celebration to be held and nationally televised the night before his inauguration. The show would include Johnny Carson, Donny and Marie Osmond, Ethel Merman, Ben Vereen, and Rich Little.

I was asked to be music director for the show. As such, it was my responsibility to find and hire an orchestra. I called my brother Tom—who happens to live in Baltimore and who is a wonderful saxophone and reed player—and asked him if he could hire the band for me. He told me that he worked for a local contractor by the name of Gene Donati, and that it would be unethical for him to hire the band without including Mr. Donati. So I hired Gene Donati, and told him that I would not have known to call him, were it not for my brother. I also asked him to remember Tom's gesture. From then on, Mr. Donati referred to himself as Frank Sinatra's personal contractor, without reference to my brother. He was awarded the same job for President Reagan's second inauguration, again without reference to my brother. Don't you just love people like that? That's life; that's how it goes.

We went to Washington in January 1981 to prepare for the gala, and Irv Cottler was still getting on everyone's nerves. Mr.

Sinatra was aware of Irv's temperament. I know that because he told me to watch out for Irv at this important function because Irv was not a show drummer. We had to play for many performers that night, and Mr. S told me that this was not Irv's forte and to look out for trouble. He wasn't kidding. As it turned out there was plenty. We had to play for Donny and Marie, Charley Pride, Shirley Verrett, and quite a few others. Irv had a tough time with much of the music, and he made life very difficult for all of us. For example, he was unable to play Charley Pride's music, and after rehearsal, he said it was crap and threw the music on the floor in a typical Irv-style temper tantrum.

In rehearsal, I was in charge of making sure all the music for the performers was properly rehearsed and that Mr. Sinatra's music was equally prepared. Even though security was nothing like it is today, it was still quite tight. We all had to pass security checks, and secret service personnel were everywhere. Talk about a night to remember! The arena was packed, and the whole night was a musical tribute to the President and Nancy Reagan.

We performed again for Nancy Reagan at a charity fundraising event held in Washington, D.C. Sinatra and Nancy were good friends, and as such Mr. S was asked to do what he could to help. As a further result of the Reagan-Sinatra friendship, we were asked to perform at the White House for the president of Italy, Sandro Pertini in 1981. Mr. Sinatra was asked to produce an evening's entertainment for this state dinner. He got Perry Como to join us, and we did a concert with both Sinatra and Como.

Attending the dinner, in addition to Sinatra and Como, were other prominent Italian Americans, such as Joe Montana and Tommy Lasorda. The night before the affair, Sinatra threw a dinner party for us and invited Perry Como and his musicians. Not only was it a great evening of sharing stories, but I also got to hang out and work with one of my musical idols, pianist and conductor Nick Perito. Nick had been with Perry forever, and he stayed with him till Perry passed away. Nick and I were asked to put together a medley of songs for Sinatra and Como to share at the performance the next night. I still have a copy of that medley signed by both Frank Sinatra and Perry Como.

The next afternoon, the day of the performance, we all congregated in the east wing of the White House for the rehearsal. It was tradition that since the White House staff didn't attend the actual performance, they were allowed to come into the room on their breaks and witness the rehearsal, which most of them did. That created a bit of a distraction for us. Under normal conditions, Mr. Sinatra didn't like having a crowd at rehearsals.

A stage had been erected for us and potted flowers had been placed all around the perimeter. Some of the flowerpots were slightly out of place or turned in the wrong direction. Mr. Sinatra was a stickler for things being in their right place, so he began personally rearranging the flowers. Perry was standing close to me and watching what Sinatra was doing. Perry seemed amazed that Mr. S would spend time on the flowers. He leaned over to me and said in my ear, "Hey Vinnie, do you think he got up early this morning and picked those flowers himself?" After the show, Perry invited us up to his suite for a drink. Those two or three days were the only time I had with Perry Como, and I will always remember him as a gracious, relaxed man with a good heart and a nice sense of humor.

One of the most charming and humorous things that took place during the evening of the performance was the reaction of the Italian president. With the exception of Irv Cottler, all of Sinatra's musicians (Gene Cherico, Tony Mottola, and myself) and Perry's musicians (Nick Perito and Bucky Pizzerelli) were of Italian descent. At the end of the show, the Italian president approached the stage and said in Italian, "I hereby repatriate all of you!" Irv didn't laugh. We all thought it was great, and I thought, wait till I tell my relatives! Before the night was over, I got to meet and shake the hand of President Reagan. What an impressive man he was. That was one hell of a great night!

CHAPTER
19
Concert for the Americas

At one point, Paramount Pictures contacted Mr. Sinatra to do the Concert for the Americas at an artist colony in the middle of a jungle in the Dominican Republic. They had built this huge amphitheater and wanted to use this concert to kick off the grand opening.

In August 1982, we flew from L.A. to Santo Domingo, the capital of the Dominican Republic. It was the epitome of poverty and filth. I stepped off the plane, walked to the bus, and immediately felt like I had to take a shower. There were dust, grime, deteriorating buildings, and broken-down cars everywhere. Shoeless kids walked through dirt streets.

A bus was waiting to take us inland to an artist colony called Altos De Chavon. The bus was quite small and very crowded. The driver told me that his friend had a small plane, and he asked if I would like to fly with his friend instead of taking the bus. Like a damn fool, I said, "Sure."

When I saw the plane, I wished I hadn't been so quick on the draw. It was an old single-engine, open-cockpit plane that looked like it had been rejected from the First World War. They started the engine by spinning the propeller. I think duct tape was holding some of the fuselage together. It sputtered, coughed, and shook, and we finally got off the ground. The pilot stayed pretty much over the beach until it was necessary to turn inland, and it turned out to be a wonderful experience to see the island and the dense jungle from the air. It took about forty-five minutes to get to our destination, and the ride wasn't half as bad as I expected, but I was very happy to be back on the ground. I felt like Snoopy flying with the Red Baron.

Altos De Chavon is a beautiful spot in the middle of the jungle. We were brought to a lovely hotel, and all of a sudden things were looking up. The next day we had to go by bus from the hotel to the concert site. The bus had to traverse a path that was no wider than the bus itself, and the foliage was rubbing against the sides of the bus as we passed through. I thought that any minute we would be running out of road. Riding with us was columnist Jim Baker of *Hollywood Reporter* fame, a fine man and a big Sinatra fan. He was there to cover the event, and it was nice to have somebody from home coming along with us.

When we arrived at the site, we were surprised to find an outdoor amphitheater where the concert was to be held. It was like it appeared out of nowhere.

We rehearsed that afternoon, and during the rehearsal, the Paramount people were filming the event and had a helicopter circling above taking shots for the TV show. That made the magnitude of the event even more impressive. I had the Buddy Rich Orchestra to work with, which was a real treat. Buddy and I got along great, and they were a good band, but they were young and intimidated by Sinatra. There was no reason for them to be, but it seemed to show. The lead alto sax player, Andy Fusco, a very good musician, was so intimidated that he got sick to his stomach. Then, during his solo, he was so afraid he would screw up that he played his sax solo out of tune.

While rehearsing, a huge bug crawled onto the stage near the piano. When I raised my foot to stomp it, Mr. S said, "Hey,

Vinnie, don't you dare, he's a friend of mine." The bug survived. Mr. Sinatra had friends in strange places.

We got everything in place, the musicians settled down, and before we knew it, suddenly it was lights, camera, action! Here's the review from *Variety*:

CONCERT FOR THE AMERICAS August 20, 1982
FRANK SINATRA,
BUDDY RICH ORCHESTRA
(Amphitheatre, Altos De Chavon)

An event like this may never turn up again in the Dominican Republic. It was not only the strength of Sinatra, who brought in the Buddy Rich Orchestra, one of the top bands today, but also the fact that this bash was the first in the five-thousand-seat amphitheatre. There have been previous concerts at Altos De Chavon, the cultural development where the amphitheatre is located. These were held on the plaza of that development, which can accommodate up to three thousand. When that proved inadequate, it was decided to build the amphitheatre.

The concert itself was an explosion, both literally and figuratively. In all instances, these two principals would provide sufficient fireworks by themselves. But following conclusion of Sinatra's final number, a fireworks display by Grucci, said to cost over thirty-five thousand dollars, kept the crowd in their seats and applauding for a full five minutes afterward.

Sinatra has rarely been better. He seemed to be having fun. He liked the crowd, which had an age range from early teens to mature elders. The audience even had a former president of the Republic applauding wildly—or maybe he was applauding his survival.

Sinatra was in great form and in excellent humor, and he communicated this feeling to the audience. There were several standing ovations during and after his turn. Vinnie Falcone conducted superbly.

Much of Sinatra's catalog was familiar, but there were two major items of interest to many. One was a new tune by Sammy Cahn and Jule Styne, "Searching," and the other was a revival of "The House I Live In," which Sinatra helped plug when he first became a name performer. His asides, incidental dancing, and repartee with the crowd gave him an ovation that can rarely be topped.

—Jose, Variety
August 25, 1982

The concert was an outstanding success and a huge crowd showed up. I have no idea where they came from or how they got there, but the place was filled. Buddy opened the show with his band. They really smoked. What a terrific bunch of guys!

However, if you ever see the video, you may notice how pale Buddy looked. After his segment, he suffered a mild heart attack and was taken away. That wasn't the only problem. Also unknown to me at the time, Irv Cottler lost his cool and had a huge argument with Mickey Rudin about me. I'm not sure what it was about, but it was probably because the orchestra was over rehearsed or underrehearsed, stayed too long in the sun, was not given enough of a break, or maybe it was just because Irv didn't like the way I looked that day. Gene Cherico overheard it all, but said nothing to me. It wasn't until our next engagement that Gene told me about the argument, because he thought that Irv would have been fired as a result. When he saw that Irv was there, he asked me if I knew what was up. I had absolutely no idea what the heck was going on, but I was to find out soon enough.

Anyway, the show was great! I've seen it many times on PBS over the years. Paramount was gracious enough to give me my own personal copy of the video of the show. When I watch it, all the thrills come rushing back.

Jimmy Cavallo, one of the original Syracuse rockers from the 1950s (now playing and living in Florida) gave this recollection:

> *I played Sunday afternoon jam sessions at the Coda in Syracuse with Vinnie. He had a trio, and they brought me in to play so any following I had at the time would bring in some additional business. It was billed as "The Vince Falcone Trio with Jimmy Cavallo." I was a Louie Prima/Bobby Darin R&B musician, and Vinnie was more Oscar Peterson jazz. I wanted to sing some other numbers, including several Sinatra songs. Vinnie wanted us to stick to just playing more of a jazz venue. I finally convinced him to let me sing the Sinatra numbers, since the audience seemed to like them. I think he just wasn't used to working with a singer, but man did he learn quickly.*
>
> *Now, fast forward ten years or so and I see Vinnie conducting for Frank Sinatra, doing the Concert for the Americas on TV. I yelled to my wife, "Geez, the last time we were together, he didn't even want to do those songs." The kid came a long way.*

CHAPTER
20

Opera Singers and Mr. S

One day I got a call from Mr. Sinatra informing me that he was going to do a performance at Radio City Music Hall, featuring Luciano Pavarotti. He instructed me to write a medley of six Italian songs, which he and Pavarotti could sing together. I included in the medley "'O Sole Mio," "Torna a Surriento," "Santa Lucia," and three other traditional Italian folk songs. We decided which parts each would sing, and I set out to put it together. The medley was to be performed with just piano accompaniment.

Pavarotti was staying in Sophia Loren's apartment at Essex House in New York City. I met Mr. Sinatra at the Waldorf Astoria, where he lived when he was in New York, and together we went to meet Luciano. He is a delightful man, full of humor and passion. We exchanged pleasantries and discussed the medley I had put together. It met with Pavarotti's approval, and we decided that we would rehearse the next day at Radio City onstage.

At some point during our visit, Mr. Sinatra asked Pavarotti's help with a vocal problem he was experiencing. I swear to you that this is true because I heard it with my own ears. Mr. Sinatra was having trouble ending certain notes at the close of a phrase the way he wanted. Normally, when a singer ends a phrase, the last note is diminished in volume and then cut off. Mr. Sinatra was having trouble diminishing the volume without his voice cracking. He said to Pavarotti, "Maestro, I'm having trouble ending a note. What should I do?" Luciano looked at him and said in the most delightful Italian accent, "Justa closa you mouth."

Mr. Sinatra literally fell off his chair, and we didn't stop laughing for a week. What was even funnier was the rehearsal the next day. We arrived at Radio City Hall about 3 p.m. The theater was empty except for us. I was at the keyboard and Mr. Sinatra and Pavarotti were standing in the crook of the grand piano as we began rehearsing the medley. The first song was to be "O Sole Mio" and was to be sung as follows: Sinatra would sing the verse, and when he got to the refrain, Pavarotti would take over. Mr. S sang the verse beautifully in his own romantic way. When Pavarotti opened his mouth and the first note came out, it was so powerful you could feel the vibration in the air. It was like turning off a transistor radio and turning on a five-hundred-watt stereo. Mr. Sinatra put down his mike, turned to me and said, "What the f**k was that?" I practically fell off the piano bench.

Mr. Sinatra loved opera singers. He had two good friends in Robert Merrill and Beverly Sills. He would often seek advice from Robert Merrill when he was having vocal problems. Merrill was always happy to oblige. Beverly the general manager of the New York City Opera and was always coming up with great venues and unique events. One day she asked Sinatra to participate in an evening of music featuring some of the greats of the operatic and classical world. Now, Mr. S was definitely not opera, but he had a great appreciation for the art. (Every good Italian should.) He said he would do it, but to his dismay, they wanted him to close the show. You've probably heard that the best act goes on last. He told me he was reluctant to close a show where some of the most powerful voices in the world would go on before him, but in the end, he agreed to it.

I hired the people we used for the New York orchestra, complete with all the trimmings, and we went to rehearsal. The New York musicians never let me down. I could always count on them, and this time was no different. Appearing on the show were Itzhak Perlman, Pinchas Zukerman, Robert Merrill, Beverly Sills, and a host of other great musical stars. The talent was beyond belief. However, as always, the audience eagerly awaited Sinatra. He and I were standing in the wings of the Met waiting to go on and listening to all that great talent perform. I said to Mr. S, "Boss, I don't mind telling you that I'm a little nervous." Without a second's delay he responded, "So am I, but that's your f**cking problem." I knew exactly what he meant. The evening went off without a hitch. Mr. Sinatra did his job; I did mine. That's the way it was with him. If you can't stand the heat...

CHAPTER

21

Working with Sinatra's Crew

Playing music for a living is a unique profession. It is an art, compounded with business. It is not like being in medicine, law enforcement, or management. Aristocrat journalist George Plimpton, who wrote *The Paper Lion* and tried all kinds of sports and activities, said that the most agonizing task he ever undertook was trying to play percussion with the New York Philharmonic. One mistake effects everybody. Playing the piano involves years and years of practice and training. It takes artistic accomplishment, a tremendous degree of creativity, and a lot of patience and perseverance; some business sense and a huge amount of common sense are also required if you want to make a good living.

Over the years I have been extremely fortunate to play with some of the best musicians in the world. Unfortunately, their egos and personalities are not always in direct proportion to their musical skill. There are those musicians who always seem to be on a cloud and easy to get along with, and then there are those who never seem to be happy, even when they are playing the best gigs. There are talented individuals who seem to be always bitching, moaning, and complaining, and others who should wear a sign on their forehead reading, "Help, my ego is out of control!" Chronic egomaniacal complainers always drove me nuts.

Once we were scheduled to do a major benefit with Mr. Sinatra in Palm Springs with all our regular guys. The orchestra was coming from L.A. where, with the exceptions of Charlie Turner and myself, all of Mr. Sinatra's personal musicians lived. The affair we were playing was an enormous charity event, and, as a result, there was a shortage of available hotel rooms. It was decided that the musicians from L.A. would come in by bus and return to L.A. after the gig. When I called our musicians to inform them of the situation, our guitarist, Al Viola, explained to me that he did not want to drive at night because of his failing eyesight. I told him not to worry, that he could ride the bus with the band. Al told me that he didn't want to ride on a bus, so I arranged to have him ride with one of the string players who had decided to drive his own car. I thought I had the problem solved.

Al then said that he didn't ride with string players and told me to get another guitarist for this engagement since it was only a one-night benefit concert. I felt that I couldn't hire another guitarist without the consent of Mr. Sinatra. I called Mr. S to consult with him. He paused for a minute and then told me to get another guitarist *permanently!* I had enough respect for Al to call him back and tell him of Mr. Sinatra's decision, and to recommend that he call and apologize. I knew that if he did so, all would be forgiven. Al's response to me was, "It's been nice working with you," and with that he hung up. I don't know what he was thinking, but he never worked with Mr. Sinatra again. Man, I couldn't believe how such a petty thing could interfere with a great job.

When I conducted for Mr. Sinatra, I seemed to have to bear the brunt of any conflict from musicians. We had extraordinary performances where everything went perfectly, and then there were nights when I had to duck from flying objects—not from the audience, but from musicians. I remember once when Mr. S forgot to introduce Irv Cottler as his drummer. After the curtain came down, Irv threw his drums off the bandstand. I was blamed for Mr. Sinatra's oversight. Cottler told me that it was my responsibility to tell Mr. S during the performance that he had been overlooked. The fact that Mr. S forgot to introduce some of his other musicians, including me, from time to time meant nothing. Irv felt he was the "main man" and told me so almost daily.

Billy May tells a great story about Irv Cottler that has been printed in several Frank Sinatra books:

> *We called Irv "Grump" because he was so congenial.*
> *He hated to be told what to do. I was conducting for*
> *Bobby Darin and Cottler was to play drums. The first*
> *date we did, Irv had a drum break in bars seven and*
> *eight of this introduction. So we rehearsed the intro-*
> *duction, and Irv played the drum break. Then Darin,*
> *who was a smart asshole kid, stopped the band and*
> *walked over to Irv and said, "Now, I'll tell you how I*
> *want this played." Irv stood up, stared down at him,*
> *and said, "You sing the songs, I play the drums, see?*
> *Don't f**k with me." That was pretty much it. Cottler*
> *was never one to hold back.*

That was a perfect example of what I was up against.

In retrospect, I must say that I rarely had trouble with the local musicians in the show bands; it was always with our own guys. I think they resented the new kid getting attention. I tried very hard to show respect to the older musicians, but after a while I just had to go straight ahead and do my job. The orchestras and I got along very well. I worked hard to gain their respect, and I think I did. It also helped that I was Frank Sinatra's conductor.

On the other hand, working with larger symphony orchestras has been both rewarding and frustrating. I have found that many symphony players don't live in the real world. They can be the most spoiled people in our industry. Many of them look down their noses at the pop end of the business, even though the pop concerts lend tremendous support to their coffers.

I will admit that many pop acts do not have challenging music, which tends to bore symphonies. In my case, however, I have had the good fortune to conduct for the best of the best, and to bring both interesting and challenging music to these orchestras. In some cases, certain symphonies were even incapable of playing the music the way I wished to have it played.

One time we were preparing for a concert with an orchestra, and after the first few minutes of rehearsing, several of the string players simply got up and left the stage. I stopped the song to see what was up. They returned to the stage with a big box of earplugs and started putting them in their ears. I was furious. I then told them that if any of them wished to leave permanently, they had my blessing. I told them that I would rather have fewer players who actually wanted to play than a section of spoiled brats. I also told them that this type of attitude was contributing to the downfall of symphonies everywhere. The manager of the orchestra came up behind me and said to me in a very soft voice, "Thank you very much."

Another instance was a trumpet player who, after I called for the orchestra's attention three minutes early, looked at his watch and gave me a dirty look. I sent him home and hired a different trumpet player. Interestingly, the great big band players rarely displayed such poor behavior. Most of the musicians in the mainstream of our end of the business are every bit as good as symphony musicians, and in many cases better. When I encounter an attitude with a pop player, it's usually because they're hiding some inadequacy. All of us have certain limitations. If your head is on straight, you recognize them and work on them for the rest of your life.

CHAPTER

22

Mr. Sinatra Has Left the Building

Frank Sinatra was a legend and a music icon, but he didn't have nearly the requirements that some of today's big-name rock groups do. His needs were not exactly simple, but if something was missing, it was no big deal to him—he worked around it. No chairs were thrown; there was no refusal to go on stage. There were no drugs, no hookers, and no tantrums.

Frank Sinatra's requirements (from his contract) were:

DRESSING ROOMS:

1 – Star Dressing Room – Frank Sinatra

This dressing room is for the exclusive use of Frank Sinatra. This room must contain a carpet, perfect and adjustable climate control, running water, sanitary toilet facilities, a shower, a full-length mirror, a dressing area, and at least four cushioned armchairs or a large couch and two armchairs. A selection of plants and flower arrangements would be appreciated.

1 – Support Act Room (Confirm number of rooms with production manager)

This dressing room is for the exclusive use of the opening act. This room must contain carpet, perfect and adjustable climate control, running water, sanitary toilet facilities, a shower, a full-length mirror, a dressing area, and several cushioned armchairs.

1 – Production Office

This room is for the exclusive use of artist's production personnel. It should contain two eight-foot tables and eight chairs.

1 – Artist's Personal Musicians and Conductor

This room is for the exclusive use of artist's musical personnel. It should be large enough to accommodate eight people.

2 – Band Rooms

Male Orchestra Dressing Room: It should be large enough to accommodate thirty people.

Female Dressing Room: It should be large enough to accommodate eight people.

Telephones

Four single, private dedicated lines: two in the production office and one in each star dressing room.

Medical Doctor

Local Promoter is to make available on call, if required on the day of the show, an ear, nose, and throat specialist with appropriate medication and sprays, including Decadron.

Frank Sinatra's Dressing Room Contents

Color TV (with second input for in-house video feed)
Upright piano
Private telephone with dedicated line, direct dial out
One bottle each:
> Mouton Cadet red wine
> Absolut or Stolichnaya vodka
> Jack Daniels
> Chivas Regal
> Courvoisier
> Beefeater Gin
> Premium white wine

Premium red wine
Bottled spring water
Large bottle of Perrier
24 Diet Coke
12 Regular Coke
Club soda
Assorted mixers
One platter of sliced fruit (to include watermelon when available)
One cheese tray (include brie) with assorted crackers
Dijon mustard
Sandwiches (two of each): Egg salad, chicken salad, sliced turkey
24 chilled jumbo shrimp
One platter of Nova Scotia salmon and hors d'œuvres
3 cans of Campbell's chicken and rice soup
12 rolls of Cherry Lifesavers
12 rolls of Assorted Lifesavers
12 boxes Ludens cough drops (cherry, honey, etc.)
One bag of miniature Tootsie Rolls
One bowl of pretzels and chips
Salt and pepper
Tea bags (Lipton or Tetley)
Honey, lemons, limes
Sugar and Sweet 'n' Low
6 bottles of Evian spring water
12 water glasses
12 wine glasses
12 rocks glasses (eight- to ten-ounce size)
4 porcelain soup bowls with knives, forks, spoons
One double burner hot plate
One teakettle with spring water
One crockpot for soup with ladle

One coffee pot, set-up with milk, cups, saucers
6 linen napkins
6 white bath towels
2 bars of Ivory soap
6 boxes of Kleenex tissues
One carton Camel cigarettes (no filter)
One bucket of ice cubes

His contract also stated, "All soda in all rooms to be seventy-five percent diet," and, "Contact Production Manager for alternatives when performing outside the U.S."

Alternatives didn't bother Frank Sinatra. He didn't care about most of the food or beverage items. We played in theaters, hockey rinks, war memorial auditoriums, and in college stadiums. Sometimes the dressing room requirements did not exactly meet the specifications requested. We went on anyway. I can't imagine some of the entertainers of today being as lenient or accommodating.

Most of the items on the list went unused. Mr. S needed the piano to warm up. I never saw him turn on a TV. I don't recall him ever asking for a doctor. He liked the bottle of Mouton Cadet red wine, used the cough drops if he thought it was necessary, and would make himself a cup of tea. He liked the Tootsie Rolls and Lifesavers. His secretary usually used the phone. If he had visitors, he liked sharing what was there. The soap and towels were just common sense, and no matter where we were working, he just wanted to make sure the facilities were clean. It could be a locker room with drapes. He didn't care. He just wanted it to be sanitary.

Mr. S always dressed impeccably: Armani suits, Rolex watches, Italian shoes, and custom-made shirts. He wanted the best, and he bought the best. His hairpieces could be a little suspect sometimes, but he was careful about that too. Mr. Sinatra was cool, and that's what he wanted people to think. A book came out a few years ago called, *The Way You Wear Your Hat* by Bill Zehme. He wrote about Sinatra's likes and dislikes, and how he lived, but I don't know if he had ever met Sinatra.

One of Mr. Sinatra's quirks was that he absolutely hated brown shoes and anybody who wore them. In fact, if he didn't like somebody, he would refer to him as "Mr. Brown Shoes."

One thing I learned from working with Mr. Sinatra was that he was always on time. If he had an appointment, he usually showed up five minutes early. That included business appointments, rehearsals, and recordings. He wanted the other party to be on time as well. If they were five minutes late, he was probably gone.

Because he had such a huge following, he also had to disappear quickly after the show was finished. The fans who tried to get to him before and after his show were fanatic. There were autograph seekers by the thousands, as well as people who just wanted to shake his hand or to touch him. It echoed his time at the Paramount Theatre in New York City in the 1950s; the only difference was Mr. Sinatra was older. His fans were older too, but another generation (or two or three) came along to see him. Screamers, shouters, and usually a fainter or two would be there before and after a show. Mr. Sinatra had Jilly Rizzo as his bodyguard always, and occasionally Jilly would hire extra guards, particularly if we were abroad. In large venues one guard could not handle all the people who wanted to shake Mr. Sinatra's hand or touch him. In venues like Radio City Music Hall, or even the Sunrise Musical Theatre in Miami, there would be many empty fifty-gallon barrels in the wings, just for the flowers that would be thrown onstage or left backstage.

Here's what Peter Graves, orchestra leader for the southern Florida band that backed up Frank Sinatra for a number of years, remembers:

As soon as the curtains closed, fans would stream to both sides of the curtain, trying to get to Frank. Vinnie would be picking up the music, I would be putting my trombone in its case, and we would just try to get back to the dressing room in one piece. One thing I remember vividly about playing at the Sunrise Theatre was that Sinatra had a helicopter outside to take him to Palm Beach, where he had friends. That was amazing. That beat any limo for any star I ever worked with. By the time his fans got backstage, he was probably twenty miles away in the air. You talk about "Elvis has left the building." Sinatra had really left the building.

I can recall many nights when, at the end of the show, I would start the bow music and then run out of the orchestra pit to join Mr. Sinatra in his limo to return to the hotel. We would be halfway back to the hotel and the crowd would still be applauding and yelling, "Encore!" He never did an encore. He gave his all at every performance, but when it was over, it was over.

One night I had put my Rolex watch in my vest pocket because it was so heavy—I didn't like it on my wrist while I was conducting. As usual, I started the bow music at the end of the show and proceeded to run to the limo to join Mr. Sinatra. As I approached the limo, I reached for my watch and found it missing. I was panicked. I couldn't keep Mr. S. waiting (nobody did that), but the watch was valued at around ten thousand dollars, and I didn't want to lose something of that value. It occurred to me at that moment that I would never see my watch again. If any of the crowd had picked it up, they wouldn't know whose it was, even if they were honest enough to return it. At that precise moment I felt a tap on my shoulder, and when I turned around, there was one of the security guards holding my watch. He had seen it fall from my tuxedo and was kind enough to follow me and return it. I never took it off again. Man, what an experience. And it was a real lesson to be more careful when leaving a show with the old man.

Mr. Sinatra was so magnetic that one time I was almost crushed to death by a crowd trying to get to him. We were in London and were to appear at Royal Festival Hall for one week and Royal Albert Hall for a second week, with two days off in between. Mr. Sinatra and I went to Royal Albert Hall on one of the days off to check out the sound and lights for the show, as well as the dressing room facilities. Somehow the word got out that Mr. Sinatra was going to be there, and when we arrived there were several thousand people. Unfortunately, there were no policemen to control the crowd. When we pulled up to the stage entrance, Mr. Sinatra got out of the car on the curbside and made a beeline for the stage door. I, like a damn fool, tried to get out of the limo on the street side instead of sliding over to the curbside and following Mr. Sinatra. The crowd rushed the limo and for a few seconds I was pinned up against the car. Luckily, I was able to squeeze back into the limo and exit the other side. I ran like hell to the stage door, and for the first time I understood the fear he told me he had experienced in his early days at the Paramount, when young girls tried to rip his clothes off to have a souvenir. I don't know how he got out of that era alive.

The only place where he seemed to feel safe was in New York City. On occasion, we would walk the streets of New York with only Jilly as a bodyguard. New Yorkers are a breed unto themselves. People would yell, "Hey Frank, how you doin'?" But rarely would anyone annoy him. Mr. Sinatra was friendly as long as he didn't feel threatened or disrespected by some idiot. He took me with him often to restaurants in New York, and generally people kept their cool and gave him his space. Being with him was thrilling because I knew that I was with one of the most recognized and important personalities on earth.

Looking back, it's hard to imagine anyone today with more charisma and ability to raise fervor with an audience. I never worked with the Beatles, the Rolling Stones, or Elvis, but Mr. Sinatra, throughout his career, achieved a level unlike anyone else. The fans' reactions on- and offstage were almost as though it was a religious experience for them. I remember one of the opening comics used to start a joke by saying: "I was out fishing in the middle of the lake one day, when Frank walked by..." That's the way people looked at him. Sometimes I remember thinking, I'm just glad to be around Frank Sinatra. When he finally "left the building," I was glad to have had the chance to be a part of all the excitement.

CHAPTER

23

It's Always Good to
Be Back Home Again

Before I started traveling with Mr. Sinatra, he appeared that one time in my hometown of Syracuse, New York, and he had arranged for my parents to attend the concert. That was certainly nice of him, but I remember thinking how much I would have liked to have been asked to go to Syracuse with him and have my mom and dad, as well as the dozens of relatives living in Syracuse, see me with Frank Sinatra. What a kick that would have been! Well, it didn't happen that time. He arranged for the tickets for my folks; I stayed in Las Vegas.

When I did start to travel with the Sinatra group as pianist, you can imagine my delight when I was informed that we were going to perform at the New York State Fair, which is held in Syracuse. The shows for the State Fair are held in the grandstand section of the racetrack. In fact, the stage is set up right on the track, and the stands seat seventeen thousand people. It was a big deal for Mr. Sinatra to be coming to Syracuse, and once my family found out that I was going to be there with the Sinatra show, they damn near wanted to buy out the whole venue. I come from a very large Italian family. They all called me and wanted front row seats (as if I could accomplish such a feat). I reluctantly asked Mr. Sinatra if any consideration could be given to them, expecting full well to be told by his office that it was impossible. But to my amazement, they all got great seats. The hometown boy was making good. Well, sort of.

I remember the show was in early September, outdoors, under a full moon and a starlit sky, with the temperature in the seventies. It was a beautiful evening and the comic Jackie Gayle opened the show with his usual very funny act. That was the good part. The intermittent sound system, however, made it not quite that funny. Besides, the crowd was not in the mood to be entertained by anyone except Frank Sinatra, and they made Jackie feel somewhat unwelcome. The sound system was cutting on and off, and the audience was starting to get the feeling that they wouldn't be able to hear Mr. Sinatra when he came out. Jackie Gayle would tell a joke, and the people at the far ends of the grandstand could not hear well enough to understand what he was saying, and they began yelling at Jackie to talk louder. It so unnerved Jackie that he cut his act short.

It was kind of amazing that just as soon as he left the stage, the sound system started working without a hitch, and the microphone connection was perfect. I don't know how Mr. Sinatra pulled that off. Maybe the sound technicians got the message that the boss wasn't going to deal with any problems. Sitting in the audience that night were New York Governor Hugh Carey, Pat Boone, Barbara Sinatra, and quite a few another notables.

When I walked out on stage to go the piano, my relatives began to applaud—man, how embarrassing. However, I was now in my glory, onstage in my hometown with the man himself. I thought I had died and gone to heaven. That is until he began to introduce the musicians and forgot to introduce me. To add insult to injury, he decided to sing "One for My Baby," which he had not done for some time. That meant that I had to get up from the piano and relinquish it to Bill Miller, who was still the conductor and would play that song, and only that song, with Mr. Sinatra. He never sang songs with just piano accompaniment unless he was in an intimate setting, which of course was not the case at an outdoor fairground.

After that he told the audience that one of the finest musicians in the country came from Syracuse: Jimmy Van Heusen. (Jimmy was the famous songwriter who wrote many of Sinatra's hit songs like "High Hopes," "My Kind of Town," and "Nancy with the Laughing Face.") Mr. S. was always unpredictable, and I think he did that just to make me realize that I had to keep my head on straight. This was not the "Frank and Vinnie" show. That was one of many lessons that he gave me by his actions, and not his words, during my time with him. I came to recognize such lessons without ever asking him what he meant. To me it was very obvious.

The evening was a huge success, and after the concert, my relatives threw a huge party for me. I was reunited with members of my family I hadn't seen in years. My uncles all gave me advice of one kind or another. But my uncle John, who had been a promoter of musical concerts in Syracuse for years and understood the entertainment business, pulled me aside and told me that I had handled myself very well in his eyes. He passed away not long after that night. I was glad that he had been able to see me perform, and I always appreciated his kind words.

As I mentioned, Governor Hugh Carey was in the audience that night, and he was getting ready to mount his re-election campaign. He evidently asked Mr. Sinatra to help him in his re-election bid because the next year I was informed that we were going perform once again in Syracuse, but this time it would be in the university's fifty-thousand-seat Carrier Dome, at a fundraiser for Governor Carey. Frank Sinatra always let it be known that he loved this country. Although he never told me and I never asked him, I believe that for the most part he was conservative and believed in the traditions set forth by our founders. As such, he would support causes and candidates that he believed in. I imagine that Governor Hugh Carey had his support, and therefore Mr. Sinatra agreed to perform for him.

By this time I had risen to the position of conductor for Mr. Sinatra, and I had control of the whole show. Mr. S invited Wayne Newton to perform with us as an opening act, and I hired a large orchestra for the event. This time, the tickets were primarily for big contributors and the affluent among the community. Of course, as Sinatra's conductor, my family assumed that I could get them whatever they wanted when it came to seats. Nothing could have been further from the truth: those tickets were like gold. Once again Mr. Sinatra came to my rescue, and my family had incredibly good seats. The Boss was there when I needed him.

The day before the concert Guido Singer, the man for whom I had worked before moving to Las Vegas, invited me to his home for a party that he hosted in my honor. When I left his employ, he warned me that I was making a big mistake and that I would regret leaving him, my job, and the big future he had envisioned for me in the retail business. Guido had quite a bit to drink the night of the party and, in a moment of weakness, admitted for the first time that he had been wrong and congratulated me on my success. That meant a great deal to me as I always had the utmost respect for him and his opinions.

I was now being recognized by the local press as the hometown boy who made good. Reporters from the local newspapers and television stations interviewed me. That notoriety, of course, added to my stature within my Italian-American family. The night of the concert, my uncle Al approached Wayne Newton and introduced himself as "Vinnie Falcone's favorite uncle" (which I'm sure impressed the hell out of Wayne). Thanks in part to my wonderful, but sometimes loud, relatives, I had a memorable night.

I've returned to Syracuse a few times since then (most

recently to finish this book with Bob Popyk). It's nice to come home once in a while. The streets look narrower than they did when I was a boy. The buildings aren't quite as tall as I remember them as a child. The nightclubs aren't quite as glamorous to me as they were when I was playing in them. Some of the neighborhoods have deteriorated, and are not quite as sharp as they once were, but home is home, and Syracuse, New York, will always have a special place in my heart.

CHAPTER

24

Playing for Sinatra Around the World

Traveling with Mr. S was an experience. Each show was important to him, and he treated each one like it was special, no matter what city or venue. Of course, we only played large venues. However, when we played large arenas, which were quite often home to sports teams, more often than not the dressing room facilities were locker rooms for the teams. Promoters would try to make them more hospitable by hanging drapes and putting in some comfortable furniture.

One night in Buffalo, New York, in the middle of winter, we found ourselves in such a locker/dressing room. It was colder than a well digger's ass in the Klondike, and there was no heat. I was already in my tux, but Mr. S had yet to dress. He asked to have a maintenance man come to see if we could get some heat. The man who arrived was a stout man with overalls, who resembled Junior Sample from the television show *Hee Haw*. When he entered the room and realized he was in the same room with Frank Sinatra, he stopped and looked at the Boss and said in his best Buffalo accent, "Hey Frank, you alright or what?" I thought Mr. Sinatra was going to choke trying to hold back laughter, and I lost it completely.

On one occasion, the travel agency gave us the wrong departure time for a trip to Cincinnati. When we arrived at the airport, our plane had already departed. The management then leased an old DC-3 World War II aircraft to take us to Cincinnati. We all piled on and took off. I was seated right behind the pilots, and at one point I heard one of them say to the other, "What the hell is going on?" He then turned to look down the aisle and saw Charlie Turner walking from the back to the front of the plane. Charlie weighed around three hundred pounds, and was causing such a weight shift in the plane that it affected the stability of the aircraft. They couldn't get the flaps level. The pilot yelled back to Charlie to find a seat and stay there. We found out that old DC-3 crashed two weeks later. Boy, you never know. Show business is something else.

Even when the traveling was easy, being away from home was hard. The days and nights seemed to meld into each other, and I would usually lose track of time. I missed my family, although Mr. S almost always let me bring my wife.

On the other hand, some of our trips were incredible. Frank Sinatra was a friend of Prince Ranier and Princess Grace of Monaco. He had known Grace Kelly before she met Ranier, and then he came to know the prince on the set of *High Society*. Because of that friendship, we were invited to perform in Monaco at the Sporting Club for a fundraising event sponsored by Princess Grace. There was a band for a TV show featuring Patrick Wayne, the son of John Wayne, which was being broadcast from the Sporting Club. I had to augment the band with strings and other instruments. I was able to hire these musicians from Paris. I had learned to speak some French while living in France and was able to communicate with the musicians without too much difficulty, but it was still not like dealing with American musicians.

The evening's festivities were attended by a who's who of European royalty, as well as a number of American and European film stars. Roger Moore, who was at the time doing a

James Bond film, was one of the more famous actors in attendance. Mr. S warned me that people of this elevated social stature were usually not the most responsive of audiences. Kings, queens, princes, and princesses just couldn't be seen showing too much emotion, especially towards an entertainer.

Mr. Sinatra's prediction turned out to be exactly the case. At one point during the performance, after a rousing rendition of "I've Got You Under My Skin," the applause sounded like the solo clapping at the end of the TV show *Laugh In*. Mr. Sinatra turned to me, tapped the microphone as if to see if it was really on, and said, "Do you think there's anybody out there?"

It would be difficult to describe the lavishness and opulence of the room we worked in. One wall of the room was all glass and looked out over the water. At the conclusion of the show, the wall of glass opened and a magnificent fireworks display began. I've not seen one like it since.

The next day I went to the Hotel de Paris, where Mr. S was staying, to meet him for lunch. From his balcony he pointed out a ship belonging to Adnan Khashoggi, who at that time was considered the richest man in the world. While we were watching the ship, which was the size of a navy cruiser, the bow opened up and out came a small powered craft to ferry people to and from the shore. It's hard to believe that some people live in that kind of luxury.

I've returned to Monaco many times since then, and I've always marveled at the lifestyle of the people there.

Traveling was difficult overseas because of the enormous distances, but the rewards were great. In addition to playing some great shows, we went on a safari and saw a good portion of South Africa when we went there to open up a new casino in 1980. We traveled from Las Vegas to New York, then on to Johannesburg via a small island refueling station off the coast of North Africa. When we arrived in Johannesburg, we took a small aircraft to Bophuthatswana where the casino was. We had now been traveling some twenty-seven hours.

As soon as we arrived in Bophuthatswana, I was told that we were to go directly to rehearsal. By the time we got to bed, we had been up for two days. Fortunately, we had brought the New York band with us so rehearsal was over rather quickly. Can you imagine the logistics of transporting a thirty-nine-piece orchestra on a trip like that?

We went to Egypt, Europe, South Africa, South America, United Kingdom, and all over this great country of ours. My wife and I never got rich financially, although I made a good living, but we saw the world. We even brought our kids on some of the domestic trips. Looking back, I am thankful to God that my wife, Connie, got to be a part of the Sinatra experience, especially since I lost her at such a young age.

One day in 1979, Mr. Sinatra told me that we were going to Egypt to perform for Mrs. Sadat at a charity event that would help the poor of Egypt. I believe Revlon was the main sponsor. Can you imagine doing a concert with Sinatra at the pyramids? We took an orchestra from England with us. It was one of the most incredible experiences of my entire life. My wife went with me, and we saw Cairo and a great deal of Egypt.

The trip was fantastic. We were to perform at the Great Pyramids at Giza. We stayed at a beautiful hotel just adjacent to the pyramids. Each afternoon we visited one of Egypt's historic treasures: the Egyptian Museum, boating on the Nile, and admiring the Sphinx. We rode camels, and met and visited with the residents of the area.

Connie and I enjoyed the trip immensely. Here's a moment I will *never* forget: On the day we visited the pyramids, we decided to enter the largest of the three and explore. We found an entrance and immediately we were at the base of a passage-way that led to the upper chambers of the pyramid. There were no steps, so you had to climb up the passageway almost on hands and knees. A string of lights hung from the top of the passageway and lit our way, but except for those lights, there was no other source of illumination.

As we found out, the electricity in Egypt failed several times a day, at least while we were there. We had reached a plateau on our climb to the top when suddenly the lights went out. We were in complete darkness. I reached into my pocket to find my lighter (like a fool, I was a smoker back then), and when I lit it to see where we were, I found that we were on a ledge and that, if we moved in the wrong direction, we would fall several feet to the level below. I also took note of a very large green insect that had landed on my arm. We waited, fully expecting the lights to be restored, but that never happened.

Just when I was really getting concerned, we heard a human voice wailing in the distance. It was the most eerie sound I had ever heard. I began thinking to myself that I was in somebody's tomb, and he was getting pissed. Just then, we saw a flicker of light coming from another passageway, and we followed the light through a short tunnel and found ourselves in the room that housed the stone casket. The light we had seen was from a flashlight held by an Egyptian tour guide who had brought his clients to see the inside of the pyramid. He was kind enough to lead us, as well as his clients, to safety.

The night of the concert in Egypt was perfect. The pyramids were illuminated and a stage was created at the base of the Sphinx. The audience consisted of elite members of Egyptian, European, and American society. As I conducted the orchestra, I was facing the illuminated pyramids, and in the distant desert, I could make out men on horseback as they checked out the scene and listened to the music. What a night! After the concert, Mrs. Sadat sent her personal envoy to thank me for coming to Egypt and contributing to the evening's festivities.

We also went to South America three times, and those trips for concerts in Brazil and Argentina were exciting and the number of people who attended the concerts was incredible. In the early '80s, Mr. Sinatra was hired to perform in Rio de Janeiro, Brazil, in the huge Maracana soccer stadium that sat approximately two hundred thousand people—the one where Pele played. Imagine two hundred thousand people! That's the size of the crowd at the Daytona 500. Our staff went ahead of us by about two weeks in order to erect a stage and install the enormous amount of sound equipment necessary to cover an outdoor venue of that magnitude. One cannot imagine how much equipment it took to make this concert happen.

When we arrived in Rio, we were met by many dignitaries. Mr. and Mrs. Sinatra were immediately involved in many social events, and I was not able to see him for a few days. I occupied my time by sightseeing with my wife. What a city! It was the best and worst of all worlds. There are so many attractions in Rio. There were several beaches to visit, and we found plenty of interesting people who just wanted to sit and talk with us. We stayed at the Rio Palace Hotel, which is on Copacabana Beach and is one of the finest hotels in South America.

The day prior to the concert, I rehearsed in the hotel with the orchestra that had accompanied us from New York. It was summer in Rio and the weather was beautiful, but unfortunately that was about to change. On the day of the concert it rained a steady drizzle, so our crew covered all the equipment with plastic sheets. The show was scheduled to begin at eight p.m. The crowd started to arrive by mid-afternoon. The stage had been erected on the playing field, and extra chairs were placed next to the stage to accommodate the "high rollers."

When I arrived at the stadium by police escort, it was still raining. I saw women in high fashion clothes with their fancy hairdos disheveled from sitting in the rain for hours on end waiting to see Frank Sinatra. It might be the only chance they would ever have to see their icon. I eventually went to Mr. Sinatra's dressing room, which was a converted sports locker room, to discuss the running order of the show. At about five minutes before eight p.m., he turned to me and asked what I thought we should do since it had not stopped raining. I told him that I thought we should wait for a while because I couldn't imagine being able to reschedule a concert of this magnitude and deal with two hundred thousand people who had waited all day in the rain to hear him sing. (We could not perform in the rain because of the musician's instruments and the sound equipment, although I believe, if not for that, he would have sung in the rain.) At the moment I finished talking we heard someone yell that the rain had stopped. Mr. Sinatra looked at me and said, "Shoot," which was my cue to get it on.

It took about fifteen minutes to uncover everything, get the orchestra in place, and pass out the music. On cue I started the overture, and when I had finished, he signaled me to begin his first song. We opened the show with "The Coffee Song" ("They've got an awful lot of coffee in Brazil..."), and the crowd went crazy. The roar that erupted from the crowd was so deafening that Mr. Sinatra could not hear the orchestra, and he completely lost his place in the music. He was simply overcome by the reception he was given. It took me a few seconds to get the orchestra back in sync with Mr. S, but once that was achieved, the rest of the concert went without a hitch.

What was completely amazing, and true without exaggeration, is that not five minutes after Mr. Sinatra walked off stage it started to rain again. I couldn't believe our luck, and as I ran off stage with the music, something caught my eye. Lodged inside the piano, under the strings, I saw a foreign object. I stopped to see what it was. It was a homemade voodoo doll. I picked it up and took it with me. Do you suppose...?

From Rio we went inland to the enormous city of Sao Paulo. We performed concerts at the Maksoud Plaza Hotel. What a place. Don Costa came with us as an opening act. He was featured with the New York orchestra. After their performance I took over for Mr. Sinatra's part of the program. Following the shows in Brazil, we went to Buenos Aries, Argentina, for some concerts where former U.S. Vice President Spiro Agnew was invited to come along. I got some face time with him, and we talked for a while. He was an interesting man.

In South America, the reverence for Frank Sinatra and his music was awesome. I met people who told me that they learned to speak English by listening to Sinatra's music. What a tribute to the man and his music!

I wouldn't have traded those experiences traveling with Frank Sinatra for the world!

CHAPTER

25

Atlantic City

Even under the best of conditions, being on the road was trying most of the time. We were living out of suitcases, and when we did one-nighters, we would finish a show, get to the hotel, try to sleep, and usually get up early the next day to catch a plane, or worse, ride a bus.

Even though I had lived in the Northeast most of my early life, I had never been to Atlantic City. Mr. Sinatra was one of the first entertainers to appear in Atlantic City when legalized gaming began there in 1978. By that time, I had become Frank Sinatra's conductor as well as pianist and, as such, got my first view of Atlantic City. I was not impressed. Resorts International was the only hotel open at that time, with Caesars following not long after. The town looked like Berlin after World War II. The boardwalk was run down, but there was hope in the air. Skinny D'Amato was an influential force in getting gambling approved for Atlantic City. He had owned the famous 500 Club, which was noted for featuring acts like Mr. Sinatra, and even more famous for having been the starting place for Dean Martin and Jerry Lewis. Skinny had great dreams for Atlantic City. He imagined it would one day become the Vegas of the east, with beautiful new hotels and most of all a program of urban renewal financed by gambling revenue.

Skinny and Mr. S were friends, and consequently, those of us associated with Sinatra were pulled into Skinny's circle. He invited us to his home on several occasions for dinner and just to hang out. The best part of going to Skinny's house was to watch the endless home movies he had taken of Dean and Jerry as they were developing their soon-to-be-famous act.

When Resorts International first opened, there would be lines of people outside the hotel stretching from the door for several hundred feet down the boardwalk just waiting to get in. The fire department had set a limit on how many people could safely be inside at one time. When the casino filled up, management had to wait until someone left in order to allow more people in. I saw people actually standing in line behind slot machines waiting for their chance to play. It was a madhouse and remained that way for some time until other hotel-casinos opened. Each time I have returned to Atlantic City over the past twenty-seven years, I've seen the growth of the gaming industry, but for the most part, the town has not enjoyed the urban renewal that Skinny envisioned.

In the early days I enjoyed the assortment of entertainment that Atlantic City provided. It was like early Vegas, with lounges open into the wee hours of the morning, and some of the legendary acts performing regularly both in the lounges and showrooms. After our shows at Resorts, I would go to see Sam Butera, Joe Barone and Lily Ann Carol, Frankie Randall, Billy Eckstine, Tony Bennett, Don Rickles, or Dom DeLuise. You get the picture. It was great fun and then we would all go to breakfast somewhere and laugh till the sun came up.

Today there are no more big orchestras in Atlantic City, very few cabaret acts, very few lounge groups, not much good music, and therefore not much work for the traditional musician. Times change; we all get older.

The Tony Leonardi Group
(Tony Leonardi, myself, and
Danny D'Imperio), ready to
hit the Big Time.

Totie Fields and me. She
was one of the funniest
ladies ever.

The White House
Reception for Italy's
President Pertini,
with President Ronald
Reagan. In the picture are guitar
players Tony Motolla and Bucky Pizzarelli, and
Perry Como's pianist and conductor Nick Perito.

Frank Sinatra doing a concert in L.A. A fan had sent a note with a pen asking for an autograph. Frank actually signed it. He had mellowed as he got older.

Discussing the Trilogy recording with Don Costa.

Rehearsing with Pavarotti, an incredible voice tha[t] Sinatra always admired.

Rehearsing at NBC and explaining how to take "New York, New York" out of the overture so it could be the featured song at the end of the show.

Inaugural gala ball for President Reagan. On the stage, from left to right, are President Reagan, Nancy Reagan, Frank, Johnny Carson, Ben Vereen, Rich Little, Ethel Merman, and then–Vice President George Bush.

Connie and I with Mr. S at his sixty-fifth-birthday party.

Backstage with the Count, getting ready to conduct the Basie Band.

Sinatra kept this picture on the piano in his New York apartment. The day I came there to rehearse and saw it gone, I knew there was a problem.

Discussing an arrangement with the Boss before a concert in Brazil.

In concert. The two bass players are Chuck Berghoffer and Gene Cherico (closest to Frank Sinatra) and drummer Irv Cottler.

Long-time Sinatra friend Jilly with us in the recording studio.

The "Blue Eyes" baseball team after playing Dean Martin's Red Eyes at 3:00 a.m. in Atlantic City. Pat Henry and Jilly Rizzo played with us.

Rehearsing with guitarist Tony Motolla and pianist Bernie Leighton. Frank Sinatra loved wearing ball caps. This cap was from the U.S.S. Nimitz.

Seeing the sheet music to "New York, New York" at NBC Studios in NYC.

Charlie Turner (trumpet), Bob Alexander and Sonny Russo (trombones), Paul Falise (tuba), Sid Cooper and Bob Steen (saxes)—all tremendous musicians.

Andy Williams and Connie. We all had a lot of fun together.

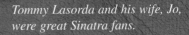

Tommy Lasorda and his wife, Jo, were great Sinatra fans.

Rehearsing at the White House for a reception for President Pertini of Italy with Frank Sinatra and Perry Como.

Relaxing with Andy Williams. I always liked being in his company.

Andy Williams is fun to be around as well as to work with.

It was an incredible treat to work with Sylvia Syms and Tony Bennett.

Tony Bennett with a baseball I had Joe DiMaggio sign for him.

Kim Gatewood pointing to the spot in the Venetian where the stage at the Sands used to be (that's where Sinatra performed).

*This is one of the sketches
Tony Bennett did of me during
a rehearsal in Los Angeles.*

Pia Zadora—a much better singer than she got credit for.

My mother and father visiting with George Burns backstage.

I'm on the marquee with The Paul Anka Show at the Dessert Inn.

Diahann Carroll, her mom, myself, and Connie. Diahann is a great singer as well as a great lady.

Connie and I with Joe and Kim Piscopo.

Myself and Eddie Fisher discussing one of his arrangements.

Rehearsing with Eddie Fisher for a recording with the London Philharmonic Orchestra

Myself with Robert Farnon, one of the world's greatest orchestrators, and Eddie Fisher.

The marquee at the Sahara when I worked there with our jazz trio.

With columnist Bob
Popyk after a Steve
& Eydie concert.
We're both from
Syracuse and have
know each other for
more than forty
years.

Backstage with The McGuire
Sisters. I don't think they
ever got older—still great
after all these years.

Playing with Debbi
Reynolds shortly
after I arrived in
Las Vegas.

*Robert Goulet and I
rehearsing at his house.*

*Robert Goulet and I
at a benefit for the USO.*

*Steve Lawrence,
Buddy Greco, and
myself—we're all
great friends.*

*I love this picture of Annette and me together.
I feel very lucky to have found her.*

CHAPTER
26

Pianos I Have Known

A saxophonist, a trumpet player, a trombonist, a violinist, and almost any other member of an orchestra have one thing in common. They can carry their instruments with them, thus ensuring that they have a quality instrument to perform on. Not so for the poor pianist. You can't stick a grand in the back of your car. A piano player has to put up with whatever is provided, and believe me, that can be a big problem.

In my younger days, I had to play on pianos that were in such horrible condition that they were virtually unplayable. At that stage of my career, the club owner would respond to my complaint by saying something like, "Hey kid, it's a piano, play the damn thing and stop bothering me!" When the club owner had a bent nose and an attitude, you generally kept any further complaints to yourself. It was out of self-defense that I made the decision to learn how to tune and repair pianos. That was one of the best decisions I ever made.

I can remember one gig in Syracuse where the piano was so out of tune that I had to play in a different key from what the other players were playing so we would all sound the same. Try that sometime!

As my career progressed and I began working for more recognized acts, the chances for a good piano improved. Most concert halls have relatively decent instruments, but no matter how good the piano is, if it isn't maintained technically and tuned properly, it will not sound good or play well. I have been asked many times which piano I prefer: I think the greatest piano in the world is a good Steinway. Because they are completely handmade, no two are alike. A Steinway that I find wonderful might not please another pianist. We all have our likes and dislikes. The Japanese and Germans also make some fine pianos. However, I personally find that many pianos being made today lack the quality that was found in the pianos of fifty to ninety years ago.

Many high quality older pianos can be rebuilt and can assume much of the greatness that they once enjoyed. Steinways in particular, if rebuilt by a highly skilled rebuilder, are often superior to a new piano. One such piano comes to mind. Just outside of Syracuse during the 1950s and '60s was a famous nightclub called Three Rivers Inn. All the great acts of the day performed there, including The McGuire Sisters, Steve & Eydie, and Bobby Darin. The club was owned by Dominick Bruno, a likeable businessman who was also in the vending machine and jukebox business. I knew Dominick very well, and he liked me well enough to ask my advice as to what piano to buy for the club when he needed to replace his old one. There was a beautiful rebuilt Steinway at Clark Music that I thought would be great for him, and he liked the price and eventually bought it. He even paid for it, which was a feat in itself. The piano was vintage 1895 or so and, in those days, pianos were built with eighty-five keys instead of the eighty-eight keys that are on modern pianos. This difference in no way compromised the quality of the piano; it was just the way that they were made in those days.

Bobby Darin was to perform at Three Rivers Inn for two weeks. On the day of his first rehearsal, I got a frantic call from

Dominick wanting to know what kind of piece of crap piano I had recommended for him to buy. I asked him what the hell he was talking about, and he told me that Bobby Darin was refusing to play the piano because it had only eighty-five instead of eighty-eight keys. When I finally stopped laughing long enough to answer him, I told him to tell Bobby that if he could show me any place in his music where those three missing keys were actually needed, I would bring him another piano and play those notes for him. I never heard another word about it.

When I was performing with the likes of Steve & Eydie, Robert Goulet, The McGuire Sisters, and certainly when I was with Tony Bennett and Frank Sinatra, it was taken for granted that a concert grand piano of high quality would be provided. In Providence, Rhode Island, at a Frank Sinatra performance once, the promoter tried to save money by not renting a concert grand piano, but instead having me use the house piano, a small white piano of dubious quality. When I saw the promoter before rehearsal, I informed him that the piano was unacceptable and did not meet our requirements as set forth in Mr. Sinatra's rider. The promoter said to me in a very condescending tone that the piano was good enough for everyone else that played there, and it would have to be good enough for me. When Mr. S arrived at the rehearsal, he asked me if everything was all right. I told him what had transpired with the promoter. All he said to me was, "Oh, yeah?" Not two minutes later, the promoter came running up to me saying, "Mr. Falcone, what is the problem? Mr. Sinatra said that if I didn't satisfy you as to the piano, he wasn't going to sing tonight." Well, guess what? You can believe that there was a nine-foot Steinway concert grand piano on that stage at show time. The power of Frank Sinatra could be very effective when it was needed.

Different pianists handle bad pianos in different ways. I heard that one of the piano players for Bob Hope came across a terrible grand that there was literally no hope for. It could barely be brought up to pitch, it couldn't be tuned, and some of the hammers were stuck. After the rehearsal, when everyone had left the theater, he rolled the piano over to the end of the stage and gave it a gentle push into the orchestra pit. They found a better piano somewhere. The satisfaction he got from that must have been enormous.

Because I learned to tune and maintain pianos from my old school master, Mr. Metzger, I believe that the old traditional methods of tuning are the best. When I see a tuner using a modern electronic scope as an aid to tuning, I liken that to a brain surgeon wearing mittens. Consequently, if and when I enter a concert hall and see a tuner using a scope, I quietly ask the stage manager to send him home and then proceed to tune the piano myself. I carry a complete set of piano tuning tools with me wherever I go.

Once in a great while, for one reason or another, it becomes necessary to use an electric or digital piano. They have really come a long way in the past few years. Recently, I did a theater-in-the-round concert with Steve & Eydie, and there was just too little room in the pit to accommodate a twenty-seven-piece orchestra and a grand piano. In that case, discretion was the better part valor, and I agreed to use a digital piano. In the past, I wasn't a fan of such instruments, but when amplified properly and played with an understanding of the instrument, a good digital piano will work.

A pianist's performance is, to a great degree, limited or enhanced by the piano on which he has to perform. If the proverbial genie could grant me one wish, I would ask for a magic wand, that, when tapped on the stage of a concert hall...*poof*...a nine-foot concert Steinway grand piano would suddenly appear. Now that would be something, wouldn't it?

CHAPTER
27
You're Fired!

Everything was going well. I loved the travel, and Mr.
Sinatra's generosity allowed my wife to come with me on some
of the longer-distance engagements. Those were great gigs—
playing experiences that all musicians dream about, even if you
aren't personally the headliner. Playing and conducting for a
headline act was my goal, and I had achieved it.

Frank Sinatra and I got along like father and son. In all the
time I worked for him, he never once raised his voice to me or
criticized how I played or conducted for him. He made it clear
to everyone how much he approved of what I was doing. I heard
these compliments from people he spoke to, but never directly
from him. Occasionally, onstage, he would praise my conducting or playing of a selection, but always quietly and directly to
me, not to the audience. However, his introductions of me to the
audience were often very flattering and to me a source of great
satisfaction. We had a terrific relationship. I didn't think it could
get any better.

So you can imagine I was more than stunned when on the
opening day of our Carnegie Hall engagement in September
1982, I was called by Mickey Rudin and fired. That was it. It
was over. I was done. I guess I should have known something
was up, because the day before Mickey called me, I was with

Mr. S in his apartment rehearsing and I noticed that the picture of him and me together, which he had kept on the piano, was no longer there.

Irv's constant bitching about me had finally convinced Mickey Rudin that something had to be done to end his complaints. Irv Cottler wanted me gone because he perceived me as taking over what he regarded as his leadership position. Don Costa told me that Mr. Sinatra had called him and asked him what he thought about letting me go. Don and Mickey Rudin advised Sinatra either to fire Irv and not me, or to fire both of us. (Both Costa and Rudin confirmed this later.)

Mickey called me at my hotel the next day and asked me to come to his New York apartment. I had no idea why he wanted to see me. When I arrived he sat me down and said, "Vinnie, things are just not working out, and after this engagement at Carnegie Hall, we're going to make a change." I was stunned. All I could think was: after seven years, things are not working out?! What a bunch of crap! If things weren't working out, it certainly wouldn't have taken seven years to realize it. Irv had gotten his way.

It was really deplorable that I was told on opening day. I had to work two weeks knowing that I was through. I was determined to go out with dignity. The next time I was with Mr. Sinatra, I thanked him for all that he had done for me. All he said was, "Oh, Mickey talked to you." After that he treated me as always, except that he didn't call me to do his vocal exercises before each show. I guess he didn't want to make me feel any more uncomfortable than necessary. He continued to introduce me to the audience each night, but not last as he had always done. He began to introduce Irv last, which I'm sure gave Irv much pleasure. Irv never said a word to me the whole two weeks, and I sure as hell wasn't going to talk to him. I was mad as hell and secretly hoped Mr. Sinatra would miss me and call me back.

One of the nicest things that happened after I learned of my firing was the response I got from the New York musicians. Almost every man wished me well and said how unfair they thought this whole situation was. But the most touching of all was the call I got from Sol Schlinger, the great baritone saxophonist, who said, "Vinnie, I have always thought Sinatra to be infallible, but this time he has made a big mistake." I don't know if I ever told Sol what that meant to me. I left New York the morning after closing night, and went back to Las Vegas to pick up the pieces and go on.

Charlie Turner, lead trumpet player, remembers:

Vinnie got fired in New York because of Irv. I was upstairs in a dressing room at Carnegie Hall and nobody could believe it. Vinnie sure as hell was doing the job. Irv got to Frank and Mickey Rudin, and Irv probably said it was either him or Vinnie. Irv got Al Viola fired too. That's too bad because Al wouldn't hurt a flea. When guitarist Tony Mottola came on board, I told him to watch out for Irv. I told him Irv was a real snake. Well, Irv found a way to get rid of Tony too. He was gone. Irv finally died in 1989. It was too bad. People said it was because of a heart attack. I don't think it was a heart attack. It was probably a broken heart. He didn't have too many friends at the end. Maybe he never knew why.

With the exception of my wife's death, those were some of my bleakest days. But all the metaphors like, "Every cloud has a silver lining," and "You don't get a rainbow without a lot of rain," kept going through my head. I needed every ounce of positive thinking I could muster. I had been fired. I was terminated from a job that had become my life. Little did I know that all of this would eventually work to my advantage.

CHAPTER
28

Picking Up Where I Left Off

It was strange not working for Frank Sinatra, but I lived. I went back to my job as house pianist at Caesars. I was happy to have a job and still be able to pay my bills. Connie was in my corner through all of this, as were my friends. You really find out who your friends are when life takes a tumble. I'm glad most of them stuck with me.

In spring 1983, I got a call from my friend Tino Barzie. He asked me if I would be interested in working with him on the career of Pia Zadora. Pia had been a one-time opening act for Mr. Sinatra in Atlantic City, which is how I met both Tino and Pia. Pia was married to Meshulam Riklis, who owned, among many other businesses, the Riviera Hotel in Las Vegas. They made me an offer I could not refuse.

Pia had been the object of many jokes about her talent, but the girl really could sing. Oddly enough, her forte was not pop or rock, but singing the standards (even though she was quite young). Tino and I worked with her for about two years before taking her on tour. I tried to help her with her phrasing and interpretation of these great songs.

Sylvia Symms (a singer that Mr. S loved) and I had become great friends. She also was a big influence on me. She advised me not to take on Pia, as she felt that people in the business would laugh at me. But after she heard what we were doing with Pia, she changed her tune. I even got Sylvia to coach Pia, and for a time she traveled with us and gave Pia the benefit of her knowledge and talent. I believe Pia improved considerably with Sylvia's help.

While I was working with Pia, I started getting calls from other singers. Andy Williams hired me for his first Christmas show tour in 1984. Since then, I have worked with Andy many times, and I consider him a friend.

Pia was making great progress, and Tino decided it was time to debut the new Pia. She did very well and continued to improve as a singer and stage performer to the point that those who had been critical of her past ventures now had to admit that she possessed great talent. I remember doing the *Tonight Show* with her. Johnny Carson apologized to her on the air about making jokes in previous monologues, and he complimented her on a fine *Tonight Show* performance.

As Pia's popularity grew, she got more work. We were on the road a great deal and Tino decided she needed security. Since Jilly Rizzo was temporarily on the outs with Mr. Sinatra, Tino asked him to join us. We traveled first class and that certainly appealed to Jilly. I think it took his mind off his problems with Mr. S, at least some of the time. It was during this time that I really got to know Jilly. He was a lot of fun, and a unique individual.

He told me stories of his time with Mr. Sinatra, and some of them were hysterical. Jilly said that one time he was holding a parking place on a New York street for Frank Sinatra's car by standing in the space. Another limo tried to take the spot, and when the driver tried to force him aside with the limo, Jilly began beating the limo with his fists and put several dents in the car. The driver got the message and backed away. Even in his later years, Jilly was a formidable physical force.

I remembered some comical stories Mr. Sinatra told me about Jilly. My favorite was the one about Mr. Sinatra taking Jilly to Bennett Serf's funeral so he could see a man who had died of "natural causes." (Not the kind of causes you see on *The Sopranos*).

I had finally become Jilly's friend, because he told me some things about what went down after I was fired. Jilly said that, two weeks after I was gone, Mr. Sinatra said to him, "I've got to get Vinnie back." Knowing Jilly, he would never have said that if it were not true.

I loved working with Pia. Tino Barzie knew exactly how to promote her. With years of experience as a manager, Tino had been Tommy Dorsey's manager until Tommy's death. He then moved on to people like Jackie Gleason and others. Sinatra Senior hired Tino to manage the career of Sinatra Junior, and for years Tino ran Junior's career. In fact, Tino was in the next hotel room when Junior was kidnapped. He never heard a thing and didn't know about it until much later.

Tino had Pia performing all over the world, as well as at many of the major venues here at home. Mr. Riklis, known as Rik, saw to it that we had every tool necessary to put Pia in the best possible light. Pia recorded albums orchestrated by the world's greatest orchestrator, Robert Farnon. We made two of them in London. The first was with the London Philharmonic Orchestra and the second was with the Royal Philharmonic. I had some of the finest music available to anyone. It was wonderful.

The challenge came afterward, when we started taking Pia's show on the road. There was no way we could travel with an orchestra of that size, yet we needed to recreate the sounds that were on the albums. It fell to me to come up with a method of reducing the size of the orchestra, yet still retain the big sound we had achieved on the recordings. I reduced the big band side of the orchestra to thirteen players, but I had to somehow recreate the sound of the string section without actually using live strings. I wanted to see if I could get the realistic sound of a string section by using a keyboard so I started experimenting with string synthesizers. It occurred to me that if I used two keyboards and split them so that one played the violin parts and the other played the viola and cello parts, perhaps I could achieve my goal. That would reduce the size of my string section by eighteen players.

I found that the Roland XP 60 or XP 80 keyboards were the best all-around instruments to give me the sound I was looking for. Working with my sound people, we were able to process the sound on stage to give us a very realistic reproduction of a live string section. I then began to rewrite the music so that the string parts could be adapted to the keyboard. I also had to find musicians with knowledge of orchestral writing sufficient enough to be able to make the Roland keyboards sound as authentic as possible.

This did not always solve our problems. After recording the first album entitled, *Pia and Phil* ("Phil" being the London Philharmonic Orchestra), we were invited to play for a gigantic music festival being held, in of all places, Cairo, Egypt.

As I mentioned, we always traveled in style. Rik owned a converted Boeing 727, totally customized and complete with a gourmet chef. In addition, he owned a small jet and a helicopter. We traveled around the world in the 727, which had been outfitted with reserve fuel tanks where the baggage compartment had been.

Pia had a recent hit song in Europe with Jermaine Jackson called "Baby the Rain Must Fall," and the two of them were very popular overseas at that time as a result of the recording. That was primarily the reason Pia was invited to the music festival in Cairo. They wanted her to perform that song with Jermaine and then do orchestral numbers we had just recorded in London. Jermaine came with us to Egypt, and the promoters told us we would be performing with the National Radio Orchestra of Egypt. Pia and Jermaine would do their song using a recorded track for accompaniment, and then Pia would do her solo performance with the orchestra.

I warned Tino about the possibility of the Egyptian orchestra not being up to our standards, but Tino told me that the promoters had been assured by the Egyptian government that the orchestra would be world-class. When we arrived for the rehearsal at the pyramids, we were given a room in the tourist reception building to hold the rehearsal. I know that there are great Egyptian musicians, but we sure as hell didn't get any of them. After trying to rehearse the first song for forty-five minutes and not getting past the first four bars of the song, I knew that we were in deep trouble. The orchestra just couldn't begin to play the music I had brought.

There were thousands of people who had come to hear this concert, and we were afraid that if we did not perform, there would be a riot. By sheer luck, Tino had brought the recorded tracks of the London Philharmonic with us. I don't know why he brought them, but thank God he did. I told the orchestra that we were going to augment their sound with our tracks. I did not want to insult them so I explained that we had recorded this music with a much larger orchestra; to duplicate that sound, we would use the recorded tracks to augment their sound. They bought my explanation, but they were also unaware that we had shut off their mikes. The audience could hear only the recorded tracks.

Since we were using the recording, I didn't have to play the piano. That worked out well because we were able to involve Jermaine Jackson in the show by having him sit at the piano and pretend he was playing. The concert was a huge success, and we laughed about it afterward. We sure didn't think it was funny at the time.

We didn't laugh for long, however, as we heard about the hijacking of the Italian cruise ship *Achille Lauro*. Terrorists from the Middle East had hijacked the ship near Egypt, and killed an American passenger, Leon Klinghoffer. After the terrorists fled, the ship docked in Egypt and the passengers were sent to the hotel where we were staying, the Ramses Hilton. All hell broke loose the next day when American military planes forced an Egyptian jet to land in Sicily because they had suspected that the terrorists were aboard.

The climate in Egypt quickly became less than friendly toward America and Americans. Although we did not personally experience any trouble, we felt it necessary to get the hell out. Thank God Rik had the plane standing by. We hopped on board and left Egypt for Germany, where we were to do a TV show. We were out of there!

29

Frank Sinatra:
The Second Time Around

From the end of 1982 to 1985, I buried myself in Pia's development. We rehearsed endlessly at her house in Beverly Hills. We became like a family—Pia, Tino, Rik, and me. Between rehearsing and recording, I had little time to dwell on being terminated by Mr. Sinatra, but I never forgot Jilly telling me that Mr. Sinatra said he wanted me back.

One day while performing with Pia at the Beverly Theater in Beverly Hills, my wife called asking if I had gotten a call from Mickey Rudin. I told her I hadn't, and when I didn't get a call the rest of the day, I forgot about it. It seems he had called my home in Vegas, and my wife told him where I was. Early the next morning, before I had left my hotel room, the phone rang. It was Mickey Rudin's secretary. He got on the phone and asked me if I would come to his office that day to talk to him, and of course I said yes.

Ironically, my hotel was just across the street from him. When I arrived I was escorted into his magnificent office. He was one of the most respected and feared entertainment lawyers in the business—probably more feared than respected.

I was treated with much more respect this time. He actually was pleasant to me. What he had to say was one of the most unexpected and rewarding things I had ever heard. He told me that Mr. Sinatra wanted me back, and that he wanted me to start immediately. I couldn't believe my ears. I had been exonerated! It was like being proved innocent or being released after a false arrest charge. I held back my joy to keep whatever negotiating leverage I had. We had to talk about money. He was very generous. Actually, he wasn't the one who was so generous, Mr. Sinatra was. I left his office on a cloud. I couldn't wait to call my wife. I was back. After two and a half years, I was once again Frank Sinatra's conductor.

The first night back it was as if I had never left. We both picked up where we left off. I approached Irv and suggested that we let bygones be bygones, but I could quickly see that nothing had changed with him. I didn't know at the time that he had been warned not to cause trouble.

Charlie Turner, lead trumpet player:

Vinnie was rehired by Sinatra two and a half years later. It made no sense that he had gotten fired to begin with. I know that Irv Cottler hated the fact that Vinnie was back, and he let everyone know. I'm sure it didn't bother Vinnie at all. That probably made Irv more annoyed than ever.

Being around Mr. Sinatra was being around the best there was. He was the Chairman of the Board. He worked hard at being the best. He showed me that devotion to music is paramount, and that you can never be completely satisfied with what you did on the previous night. He used to say to me that when we were not great, we damn well better be very good. I've never forgotten what he taught me, and I never will! I will spend the rest of my life passing along his teachings to those who are interested in making great music.

The first engagement after being rehired was in 1985. It was a tour that started in the Midwest and was to end in Florida.

My friend Peter Graves, a trombonist from Miami, was hired to contract the band for the entire tour. Peter and I had previously worked with Sinatra on many occasions, so I knew I would have an excellent band. I say band instead of orchestra because on this tour we were not using a harp and string section, but a big band configuration. We had used the smaller group in the past when it became necessary because of logistics.

At the first rehearsal, I noticed that many changes had been made to the music. My friend Joe Parnello had taken my place after I was fired. He saw how Irv had caused my demise, and he didn't want the same thing to happen to him. For one reason or another, Joe and Mr. Sinatra didn't get along musically, and that led to a strained personal relationship. On top of that, Joe had to deal with the pressure put upon him by Irv. Joe told me of the difficulty he was having. Irv was trying to run the show, and it was getting impossible for Joe to control the way the bands played the music.

Instead of just insisting that the music be played the way it should have been played, Joe started to make changes in the charts to get what he thought Mr. Sinatra wanted. He did this to avoid looking like he was usurping Irv's power. I know exactly what he was experiencing. Joe thought that by coddling Irv, he would be safe in the job. What he didn't realize was that just the opposite was happening, and that is why Mr. Sinatra hired me back. I felt terrible for Joe when he was fired. I had been there.

I now was faced with putting the music back the way it was supposed to be. Gene Cherico and Charlie Turner had been replaced in my absence. Gene's replacement was bassist Don Baldwin, who had never played the music in its original form. When I started reversing the changes that had been made and Don played them for the first time, he questioned me and told me that this was all wrong. I had to remind him, and the rest of the band, that I had come to know this music inside and out as was taught to me by the man himself, and they would now please do it "my way."

I had no further problem with Don, or for that matter Irv, who had been told if he caused trouble this time he would be out. (Mr. Sinatra and Mickey Rudin told me this later on.) Mr. Sinatra did not come to the rehearsal that first day, which pleased me. I felt it showed that he was confident that I would have things right for him, even though I hadn't been with him for almost three years.

When I went to Mr. Sinatra's dressing room that night to prepare the lineup for the show, he greeted me as if we had never been apart. He came over, pinched me on the cheek (a nice little Italian thing that you see in *The Godfather* movies), and asked if everything was okay. Then we got down to business.

It seemed like I had never left. We went to work, as always, laying out the music on the floor to decide in what order the show would be performed. Then, by looking at the titles, he could see if the pacing was to his satisfaction. Once this was completed, I would go onstage and have the orchestra put the music in the order that we had decided. The show was a smash.

The next day I was speaking with Hank Catania, Sinatra's sound and light engineer. Hank had joined Mr. Sinatra after I was fired, and he told me that, for the first time since he had joined the crew, Mr. S had good things to say about the show. I was overjoyed.

When we finished the tour, we came back to Las Vegas. At this point, Mr. Sinatra had switched from Caesars Palace to the Golden Nugget, where we were scheduled to perform next. I went to rehearsal eager to reunite with my friends who made up the Las Vegas orchestra. I was in for a real surprise. The configuration of the string section had been radically altered, and once again I had to straighten things out. I spent a great deal of time working on the ballads, trying to get the shadings the way

I knew he wanted them. On top of that, playing the Golden Nugget wasn't the same as playing at Caesars Palace. In fact, it was a real letdown. The room we played in was a converted ballroom with poor acoustics.

When the orchestra and I were satisfied, we rehearsed "For Once in My Life," a real swing number with the orchestra at full tilt. Mr. Sinatra had quietly come into the room without my knowledge and had walked up behind me. We started the song and the band was smokin'. Suddenly I heard his voice behind me. "Yeah, Vinnie!" he roared. I knew I was home again.

After Vegas, we went to New Orleans. Joe Williams, the premier vocalist from the Basie band and a truly great artist, was performing at the Fairmount, and we all went to see him. Irv and I had been cordial up to this time, but when Joe Williams introduced me and did not mention Irv, things started turning for the worse again. Irv started with the same old crap. He just never learned.

I was back working with Mr. Sinatra, and in my glory once again. I was also still working with Pia Zadora. After several months, I was told that Mr. Sinatra wanted me to devote all my time to him, and that he wanted me to be available whenever he wanted me. I was faced with a monumental decision. What a dilemma. Do I go back with Sinatra, or do I stay with Pia? Pia's career was still in its infant stage, and I had no trouble juggling my schedule at first.

I called Mickey Rudin and told him to relay to Mr. Sinatra that I couldn't risk putting my neck back in the noose, so to speak. I explained that I had a family to support, and that I needed to keep all of my options open. I couldn't afford for Irv or anyone else to get me fired again for any reason. I asked that Mr. Sinatra allow me to work with both him and Pia concurrently, and when (and if) I had a conflict, Bill Miller could return and do the performances that I couldn't.

I fully expected him to say no, but to my surprise, he agreed. Bill Miller came back, and once again I had the great pleasure of working with him. However, this time our roles were reversed. To Bill's credit, he never complained or said anything to me. We worked together as a team. Bill Miller is truly a talented, warm, decent individual. I don't think anyone has ever said a bad word about him.

Things were fine for a while, but Cottler was still driving me nuts. In fact, he was driving everybody nuts. On top of that, I was getting busier and busier with Pia. I finally wrote Mr. Sinatra a letter explaining once again that I had to maintain my independence. I reminded him that he was the one who had taught me the importance of that. I cited the example of when he left Tommy Dorsey to strike out on his own. He must have understood, because he never held that against me.

As a result of my decision not to work for him exclusively, we parted ways, though we were to work together again. I never looked back, and I know that I did the right thing. I have been told that I am one of the few, if not the only one, to separate from the Sinatra group the way I did and still remain on his good side.

From that time until my last meeting with him, he was always most gracious and friendly towards me. He even supplied a wonderful quote for the liner notes of an album I recorded in later years.

Frank Sinatra Jr. assumed the role of conductor for his father. Shortly after, I had the opportunity to help him out. One night Frank Sinatra Sr. wanted to sing "My Kind of Town," and Junior realized he had forgotten to include it in the music case. He was beside himself waiting to be yelled at by his dad. I had an idea that saved the day. I called the librarian Terry Woodson, who was in his Hollywood office. I had him fax each piece of music and I put them together as he was sending them. I delivered the last piece of music to the bandstand as Sinatra Sr. was introducing the song. I thought Junior was going to kiss me.

CHAPTER
30
Making a Living Without the Boss

Making a living was never a problem for me. I knew I could always put food on the table one way or another. Between the time I left Mr. Sinatra and when I was hired by Tino Barzie to direct Pia, I did very well in Las Vegas. I was back working at Caesars Palace, as well as doing casuals around town. When Tino hired me, I left Caesars forever. Life was good with Pia. By the time I was rehired by Mr. Sinatra, she was beginning to get some very good bookings. Tino was a genius at marketing Pia, and he had the full support of Mr. Riklis, which was substantial.

After the gig in Egypt, Tino put her on tour. We started playing the big venues. To give her some drawing help as she became better known, Tino hired such big stars as Norm Crosby, the great French singer Charles Aznavour, Rip Taylor, Jack Carter, Jackie Gayle, and Phyllis Diller to share the bill.

Rip Taylor and Jack Carter became my friends. What a pro Jack Carter is, and a funnier man than Rip Taylor just doesn't exist. Charles Aznavour is magic onstage, and he brought a new dimension to the show. He is the Frank Sinatra of Europe, and he has a huge following in the U.S. among the French-American population, and especially among the Armenian people who live in North America. Charles and I became friends, and in later years, he hired me to be music director for all his North American tours.

Pia had somehow caught the eye and ear of Barbara Bush, and when President George H.W. Bush was running for office, we were asked to perform for several campaign functions. Once we did an outdoor function for vice presidential candidate Dan Quayle. The band was on a makeshift stage, and secret service agents were everywhere, passing by the band regularly. I remember asking one of the agents politely if he would please be careful when he passed by the saxophones so as not to knock one over and damage it. I was told quite impolitely to mind my own business and shut up. Being the hot-headed Italian that I am, I told this man that the last time I checked this was still a democracy, and I could tell him anything I damn well pleased. What a great country!

The next thing we knew we were invited to perform for President George H.W. Bush's inaugural celebration. Once again I got to participate in one of our nation's proudest traditions. He came onstage with us and shook my hand. I was now two for two, first Reagan and now Bush. (Four years later, I did President Bill Clinton's inaugural celebration with Tony Bennett.)

Meanwhile, Pia was becoming less and less enamored with her blossoming career. She really wanted to sing rock music. She made two rock albums without Tino's or my musical participation, one with Michael Walden and another with Jimmy Jam and Terry Lewis. Neither was a success.

It was a shame that Pia wasn't more interested in performing the great American standards. At the time of her first two recordings, she was the only other female singer besides Linda Ronstadt doing that style of music. I believe that if she had stuck to it, she would have had a fine career. She was, in fact, very good. After she quit, it seemed that every singer in the world tried their hand at singing the standards. Very few succeeded.

We were in Florida at the Coconut Grove doing a musical play called *Too Short to Be a Rockette*, when things really started to deteriorate. The play was produced by Gary Smith, one of Hollywood's most respected producers. To choreograph the show, Walter Painter was hired; Walter is one of the best choreographers of Hollywood and Broadway.

Pia was getting tired of the show and was beginning to not listen to Tino and me. I gave my notice to Tino and Rik, but they convinced me not to leave just yet. Rik and Tino had always been very generous to me, and I felt obligated not to leave them in a lurch. I stayed on for another year, and I'm glad I did because it gave me the opportunity to work with Mr. Sinatra again.

In fall 1991, Tino Barzie, Pia's manager, came up with a brilliant marketing idea: Pia's husband owned the Riviera Hotel in Las Vegas, and Tino was in control of special entertainment and devised a plan for New Year's Eve 1991 that would be the end all of New Year's Eve entertainment events in Las Vegas. It would feature Frank Sinatra and Pia Zadora doing shows at the same time, in different rooms in the hotel. At nine p.m., Mr. Sinatra would be in the showroom and Pia would be in the ballroom, and at midnight, they would switch rooms for the second show.

As music director, it was my responsibility to hire two large orchestras to accompany each star, as well as to orchestrate the switch from room to room. In addition to conducting one orchestra for Pia's show, it was necessary to arrange the transfer of the key musicians for each act from room to room. I arranged for elevators on hold at specific times, security guards to accompany each group of musicians, and food and drink catering for each dressing room.

For a large amount of money, guests could eat and drink to their hearts' content and see two great shows featuring two of the best orchestras one could ever hear, and some of the greatest music ever written without leaving their seats. The night was a huge success. To this day, I believe that it was the biggest event ever staged in Las Vegas for a New Year's celebration.

Meanwhile, Pia became less and less interested in devoting herself to the work. Tino had arranged for Pia to join a tour with Frank Sinatra and Don Rickles. Tino and I felt that being in the presence of Mr. S would help to reinvigorate her.

Our first night with Mr. Sinatra, he called me into his dressing room and told me that Pia had "sung her ass off." What a compliment to Pia, Tino, and myself. Pia never seemed to appreciate the position she was in. I don't think she ever became enamored with the music she was singing, even though she was doing it beautifully. I think she always wanted to do the music more closely associated with her generation. We stayed with Mr. Sinatra until the tour ended. Shortly after the conclusion of that tour, both Tino and I left Pia Zadora.

CHAPTER
31
Memorable Performers

Through the years I have had the great pleasure to work with and get to know some of the greatest artists of a bygone era of entertainment. Some of the performers have become my friends and a great source of support throughout my career. Many of these relationships are a direct result of conducting for Frank Sinatra.

I previously mentioned Paul Anka, hit singer from the '50s, and legendary songwriter (the writer of the Johnny Carson *The Tonight Show* theme)? Well, the day after Tino and I left Pia Zadora, we went to Atlantic City to meet with Paul Anka. Paul was looking for a new manager and music director. I had known Paul casually for some time but had never worked with him. He is a great showman and gives his audience more than their money's worth. We talked and Paul said that he would contact me. I returned to Las Vegas, and true to his word, Paul called me a couple of weeks later. He offered me the job, and I agreed. Tino was also hired to be Paul's manager. Paul had decided that he wanted to do more big band music, written primarily by Don Costa, and he wanted me to reshape the orchestra and bring my experience to his show. At least that's what I thought he wanted.

I'm still not sure why, but after a while, it seemed that Paul wanted to go back to what he was doing before my arrival. Tino was not getting along with Paul either, and before long we decided that it would be best to separate from Paul. Tino left somewhat before I did. Everyone always thought that I left as a result of Tino's decision; that was not the case. I left because I wasn't able to do for Paul what I had wanted to accomplish for him musically. It was best for all concerned.

Since then, my son Danny has become Paul's lead trumpet player. Paul seems to love Danny's playing, and I couldn't be happier.

Frank Sinatra often referred to Tony Bennett as "the best singer in the business." Having worked as Tony Bennett's pianist and conductor is one of the jewels in the crown of my career. I can't tell you how I enjoyed being with him. Joe La Barbera was Tony's drummer when Ralph Sharon, Tony's great pianist for so many years, fell ill. Tony told Joe to call me. I was available and eager to play for Tony, so I accepted immediately.

Tony works with a trio or quartet most of the time. As such, all of his musicians know the music by heart, and there was little or no written music for the show. I had to learn it all by listening to tapes of previous shows and I only had a few days to do it. I stayed with Tony until Ralph was well enough to return, but it wasn't very long before Ralph fell sick again and I was asked to return once more. Over the next few years, I would either be called to play piano or to conduct whenever Tony appeared with an orchestra.

At one point, Tony offered me a job on a permanent basis, but Ralph was my friend, so I told Tony that I would love to work with him, but only after he and Ralph had terminated their relationship. I continued to play and conduct for Tony on a part-time basis. He is, without a doubt, one of the greatest performers of all time. I had the pleasure of conducting the orchestra for part of his tour with Diana Krall and with many of the best American symphony orchestras.

While I was traveling with Tony, he was invited to appear on *The Today Show*. We did two songs and then Katie Couric interviewed him about his painting. Tony is a terrific painter, and he brought along a portrait of Mr. Sinatra that he had painted. The painting was shown on TV during the interview, and I was quite taken with it. After the show, I remarked to Tony how much I loved the work. Three days after I returned home, a Fedex truck pulled up in front of my house, and the driver handed me a package from Tony. It was the painting. He has also drawn three pencil sketches of me that I proudly display on my wall. Tony will go on forever.

One of my favorite people is Sid Caesar. Sid is a jazz aficionado and a true genius at comedy. He would come into the lounge at the Sahara while I was playing there with the jazz organ trio. He would sit for hours listening to us and never say much. He appeared to be much more reserved offstage than onstage. In his act he would often do his famous bit of pretending to speak any language by using the dialect with made-up words. One afternoon he came to hear us play, and during one of our breaks I related to him my amazement that he could emulate so many languages. He immediately started speaking fake Japanese to our audience, tossing in an English word once in a while. It was hysterical, and soon everybody within earshot was laughing.

Have you ever heard Diahann Carroll perform in person? Diahann is one of the most beautiful and talented women I have ever known. She was a favorite of Frank Sinatra's. Her manager, Brian Panella, had become aware of my separation with Sinatra. Brian thought I might fill the bill, so he called me to do a cruise with her. I was also invited to bring my wife. How could I say no? I'm sure happy that I went because my professional relationship with Ms. Carroll blossomed into a friendship, and I have come to do a great deal of work over the years with this wonderful woman. Because she is such a fine actress, she understands how to interpret the lyrics of the great American composers. Couple that with an exciting voice and you have one of the best.

On one of the cruises with Diahann, we ran into a real problem. The band on the ship was from Poland, and they were totally unequipped to handle the style of our music. In addition, only one or two of these men spoke any English, and my Polish was a bit rusty—in fact, it was nonexistent. The only saving grace was the determination of these men to learn the music as best they could. They had to play dance music each night until midnight, but they came to me and offered to rehearse each night after midnight for as long as necessary. The cruise lasted ten days, and we were not scheduled to perform until the seventh night. Every night for the six nights prior to Diahann's performance we rehearsed into the wee hours of the morning. I knew that it would never be what I wanted musically, but these men were so determined and so proud to be playing the music of a great star that I just had to let them try.

Diahann is a consummate pro, and the night of the concert she just went straight ahead no matter what was happening behind her. The band played as well as they had ever played, and the audience, sensing what was happening, gave us a standing ovation. I have never seen a prouder bunch of musicians than those gentlemen, for just having gotten through the show. They thanked me profusely for giving them that opportunity. I don't know many other entertainers who would have put up with what Diahann had to that night.

Another hit singer from the '50s and '60s that I thought was great was Rosemary Clooney. I only worked with Rosemary once. Her drummer, Joe Cocuzzo, and I wrote a song as a tribute to Frank Sinatra called "The Singer." Joe had written the lyric originally as a narrative poem and sent it to me to read. I asked him if he would like me to try to write a melody to it, and he told me that it had already been tried and the other attempts didn't please him. I decided to give it a try.

When Joe heard my melody, he immediately liked it, and we decided to see if Tony Bennett would consider recording it. Joe had been Tony's drummer years ago and knew him pretty well. Tony said he loved the song, but didn't feel it was right for him at that time. Joe and I were shocked by Tony's response because we knew how much he loved and respected Sinatra. But life goes on.

Since Joe Cocuzzo was also Rosemary's drummer, we decided to give it to John Odo, who was her music director as well as our friend. John loved it and played it for Rosemary. She immediately decided that she was going to record it on her next album, which just tickled the hell out of Joe and me. I offered to go to L.A. when she was recording the album and accompany her. We knew Rosemary would sing the song magnificently, and we wanted to be there to make sure the piano track matched her rendition and that it was played the way we had envisioned it.

I took my son Jeff, who is a drummer, to the studio with me so that he could witness firsthand a legend at work. Rosemary was aware of who I was, of course, and we went into the studio to rehearse it a few times before recording. She nailed it right away and after two or three run-throughs, we began to record. In one single take, she captured all that Joe and I could have wanted. She was most gracious, and thanked me for bringing her such a wonderful song. I added the strings later and was gone in less than two hours. What most rock bands can't do in weeks, she did in minutes. The song was released on her album entitled *Sentimental Journey* from Concord Records.

I think Tony Danza is one cool guy. I knew Tony Danza before I started working with Steve & Eydie (who are also friends of his). His pianist-arranger Lenny Lacroix and I are buddies. Lenny gave me the nickname "Il Duce" (the leader), and I gave Lenny the nickname "Knuckles." Tony has matured into an accomplished performer and he captivates his audience. I don't see Tony that often, but when I do, it is just like we were together a few days ago. I guess it's an Italian thing.

One of the performers that sticks out in my memory is Sammy Davis Jr. George Rhodes was Sammy Davis' conductor and, for a time, the great pianist Paul Smith was Sammy's pianist. There was one engagement when George was unable to come to Las Vegas because of an illness. Paul Smith took over as conductor, and it fell to me to play piano for the shows. However, when there was a song that Sammy sang with only piano accompaniment, Paul would come to the piano and take my place. For those tunes, there was a chair for me to sit on to the rear of the piano. One night when I got up from the bench to take the chair, Sammy said to the audience, "Look, a white guy is going to the back of the bus." It was totally impromptu, and I laughed so hard that I almost fell off the chair.

Remember Eddie Fisher? Sometime in 1995, Tino Barzie called me and told me he had a new project developing. Tino said Eddie Fisher was looking to make a comeback and that he was going to manage him. The first thing we did was meet with Eddie and his wife, Betty, at their home in San Francisco. We all got along very well. Betty was of Chinese decent, and had become a very successful businesswoman in the U.S. She was prepared to fund Eddie's comeback attempt, and the first project was to do an album of great songs. This is where I came in. I was to help Eddie learn the songs and conceive the arrangements. We contacted arranger Robert Farnon, and he agreed to do the orchestrations. We had decided that, when we were ready, we would all go to London and record with the London Philharmonic Orchestra.

I spent the next two years working with Eddie, both before and after the recording. Farnon wrote some of the most astounding arrangements, and after recording them with him in London, Tino and I spent the next several months augmenting the tracks with instrumental solos by myself and some of the great L.A. players. We got our friend Lee Hershberg, a recording genius, to refine the sound, and we spent weeks putting Eddie's voice onto the tracks. Eddie had sung live to the tracks in London, but we needed to improve his performance for the finished product. Eddie has always been infamous for his difficulty with musical meter (knowing where to put the singing notes in relation to the music). I spent untold hours working with him, and the finished product was, in my opinion, the best singing of his life. Robert Farnon agreed when he heard the final cuts.

Tino proceeded to book Eddie for a road tour that was to start at Carnegie Hall. For a warm-up, Tino booked Eddie to sing for an affair held at the Beverly Hilton Hotel that would be attended by many of Eddie's show biz peers. Eddie couldn't handle the pressure, the concert was a disaster, and that ended his comeback. The album was never released, which is a monumental shame, and Eddie has not returned my phone calls since.

Speaking about singers from the 1950s and '60s, Connie Francis is still played on every *Music of Your Life* radio station. My friend Frank Fiore, who was managing Connie Francis, called me in the mid-1980s. He asked me to join them as her music director. That was a new experience for me because I had never been involved with someone who sang the '50s style of music for which Connie was famous. "Who's Sorry Now" and "Where the Boys Are" weren't my cup of tea. Connie and I had lunch together in Beverly Hills, and she told me that she had a nice tour coming up and would like to have me aboard. I liked her right away and agreed to take the job.

Connie's show was something unique for me. It involved videos, click tracks (synchronizing music performance to pictures), as well as a cast of backup singers and dancers. I had to learn to coordinate the music with the videos and the click tracks and keep all the parts in time. It really prepared me for things to come later in my career.

We were in Toledo, Ohio, when Ms. Francis got into a beef with the theater owner and refused to go on. The theater owner then locked us out and for several days. We couldn't get our musical instruments, wardrobe, and equipment. Finally after a few days of negotiation, we retrieved our belongings and left town. Not an easy gig.

Connie has a way of making her audiences feel like they are family, and they simply adore her and accept her unconditionally. I still conduct some of her shows. She has grown older gracefully and continues to command the stage.

Another outstanding singer I get to work with regularly is Robert Goulet. Robert is a man's man and a great voice. I have been his pianist and conductor for the past four years. He's not known as a singer of jazz material, but he is one of the few singers for whom I've ever played who can sing "Lush Life," one of the most difficult jazz ballads, and do it justice. Recently, we performed at one of the casinos in Reno, Nevada. Robert did what few singers these days can do. He sang two shows a night for four consecutive nights and packed the room each and every show.

He's got one hell of a temper, but then so do I. I've seen him go head-to-head with members of the audience who cause a ruckus or get out of hand. Usually (actually always) the audience sides with Goulet, and he comes out the hero.

There are singers who have great range and ability, and then there is Jack Jones. Jack is a pianist's dream. When I first came to Las Vegas many years ago, I heard Jack when he was appearing at Caesars Palace. I was dumbfounded at this man's vocal ability. His range is extraordinary. He loves to experiment harmonically and has the ability to improvise at will. I had met Jack a few times; but my friend Mike Renzi, a great pianist, asked me to sub for him one day in 2001 and I got to work with Jack. Since then I have worked with Jack quite often. I love playing for him as he offers as much freedom as possible for an accompanist.

I'm glad I got to cross paths with Henry Mancini. Hank has composed some of the world's greatest hits like "Days of Wine and Roses," "Charade," and "Moon River." Once I was playing and conducting for Andy Williams for a show he was doing in Beverly Hills. Hank was in the audience and Andy called him up to play piano while he sang "Moon River." Hank sat down, turned to me and said, "I don't remember the changes." He wrote the damn tune!

I love Ann-Margret. Ann-Margret is a genuine person and incredibly good-looking. In fact, she's one of the most beautiful women who ever walked onstage. Donn Trenner was her conductor and pianist. When I played for her while Donn was conducting, every once in a while she would pass me by at the piano and whisper, "Boy, are you good." I would get goose bumps.

I can't possibly forget to mention Dino. Dean Martin is one of the most unique, funny, talented entertainers I have ever met. The friendship and playful rivalry between Dean Martin and Frank Sinatra is legendary. One time, while we were performing at Resorts International, the two held a charity baseball game in nearby Absecon, New Jersey, at three a.m. I played for Sinatra's team, Blue-Eyed Entourage, and we battled to an eighteen-to-eighteen tie against Dean's team, Red Eye Express. Baseball star Tommy Lasorda was even there!

Mr. Sinatra asked Dean Martin to be part of the Reagan inaugural TV special in 1981. Dean had recently lost his son, and he was in a depressed emotional state. Mr. Sinatra realized that Dean was in no condition to perform and scratched him from the lineup.

Dean's pianist and conductor, Ken Lane, confided in me that he was extremely concerned about Dean's emotional condition, and asked me to inform Mr. Sinatra of the situation. (Dean and his musicians hadn't worked in several months.) I told Mr. S about this when we got back home. Mr. Sinatra went to Dean's house some time later and said, "Get your ass out of the house and come on the road with us." The Boss told me that Dean had expressed doubt that the public would still be interested in seeing him perform. However, Mr. Sinatra won out, and Dean ended up going. We toured as the old "Frank & Dean Show" for the next several months. The audiences loved Dean and, as a result of their enthusiasm for him, his state of mind improved rapidly.

I like Al Martino's voice. Al plays Las Vegas frequently. He called me once and asked me to conduct for him on an upcoming engagement, and I agreed. I had to learn a new show from scratch, and as a result I got to know him on a personal basis. Al had played Johnny Fontaine in *The Godfather*, which many people thought was a caricature of Mr. Sinatra. There was a rumor that the Boss asked him not to take the role; I asked Al about it, and he vehemently denied it. Al is a great cook, specializing in Italian dishes. He told me he works a lot in Germany and appears there so much that he has a home there. I asked him why Germany and not Italy? He said, "Are you kidding? In Italy, everybody's a singer."

I could never forget Phyllis, Dorothy, and Christine McGuire—undoubtedly the best female vocal group ever. When I was still playing piano in Syracuse, the sisters came in one night to hear Anna Marie Genovese, the singer I was accompanying at the Coda. I was asked to join them at their table, and I was introduced to them as an up-and-coming pianist. Phyllis had come that evening with Sam Giancana. I had no idea who he was, but I'll never forget him. When he shook hands with me, something told me that this was a man I should say hello to and then get the hell out of the conversation.

It was ironic that I would eventually conduct for The McGuires. Tony Riposo (also from Syracuse) was their pianist and conductor at the time and had worked on the road with the McGuire Sisters for many years. Finally, he decided not to travel anymore. He moved back home to Syracuse and began teaching at Onondaga Community College and working at the Syracuse CBS affiliate.

Phyllis McGuire called him one day and said they were putting together a new show. She asked if he could come to Las Vegas to rehearse with them. Tony told her it was just too far for him to travel, but he knew that I was available during the day. Tony called me, and I agreed to do it. I have performed countless shows with them over the years, including a recent PBS television special. Phyllis lives in Las Vegas, and we see each other frequently.

Did you know Joe Pesci is more than a movie star? Joe Pesci's close friend Tommy DeVito, who was once with Frankie Valli and the Four Seasons, is an old friend of mine. I met Joe through Tommy.

Joe is also quite a good singer and has recently recorded a CD. In fact, he started out with Joey Dee and the Starliters, working his way around as a waiter and singing and playing guitar in local nightclubs. When you think about Joe Pesci, you think of the mob wise guy screaming, "I'm funny how? Funny like a clown? I *amuse* you? I make you laugh?" in *GoodFellas* or the tough Brooklyn lawyer talking about "these two yoots" in *My Cousin Vinny*. Every once in a while I see him when he shows up at one of my performances.

George Shearing is a great musician and performer. Frank Sinatra selected Shearing for concert dates where he felt it wasn't appropriate to have a comedian as a warm-up act. For me it was particularly delightful because I got to study Shearing's artistry close up. At that time, George was working primarily as a duo, along with bassist Brian Torff. Mr. Sinatra wanted more than a duo so he had George add drummer Grady Tate. After a short time, Mr. Sinatra suggested he recreate the original George Shearing Quintet that included guitar and vibes. George didn't like the idea, but gave in. It was a thrill to hear the quintet again.

Because George is blind, one night comic Pat Henry came up behind him and put his hands over George's ears and said, "Guess who?" Shearing thought it was very funny.

Working with Frank Sinatra, I also got to know Frank Sinatra Jr. I think he is a very good-hearted person. I can only imagine what it must be like to be the son of a legend. We worked side by side when Pia was touring with Frank Sinatra Sr. and Frank Jr. was conducting for his father. One night, he and I had a light-hearted conversation in a backstage dressing room. During the course of the conversation he said, "Do you have any idea how difficult it is to be Frank Sinatra Junior?" I looked at him and said, "Let me be Frank Sinatra Junior and I'll show you how to do it." He had big shoes to fill.

Another "Frank" I got to know is Frankie Valli. When Frankie Valli is appearing in Las Vegas, I enjoy meeting with him. He's a friendly guy and a fine performer who has kept improving through the years. His show is a classic and just gets better. If you are ever in Vegas and have a chance to see him perform, you will not be disappointed.

"Gorgeous" is the word that best describes Raquel Welch. Raquel has appeared at Caesars Palace where she had a night-club act for a while. When she came onstage in her blue-sequined Bob Mackie gown, she took your breath away. As part of her show she did a number in which she portrayed a singer in an Old West saloon, and she dressed in a costume reminiscent of the times (like Miss Kitty from *Gunsmoke*). For that number I dressed as a saloon piano player with arm-garters and a visor-style cap, and played an old upright piano that was pushed onstage in front of the curtain. She did one tune with just me playing. The bit became a lot of fun for the both of us. About halfway through the two-week engagement, I was required to do a one-night show with Mr. Sinatra. I had to get a substitute for that evening, and teach the sub the upright piano bit. While at the Frank Sinatra performance, a messenger with a box appeared, calling my name. He gave me the box, and when I opened it, I found a T-shirt inside that had the words "Welch Aid" on the back and a note that read, "Where the hell are you?" signed, "Raquel."

Another singer I am happy to work with is Andy Williams. I got to know Andy when I was house pianist at Caesars Palace. Andy was one of the regulars at Caesars. His show was always a big production and very entertaining. He is another of the really great singers of our time. After I had left Mr. Sinatra the first time, I went on the road with Andy's new Christmas show. This was the winter 1984. We traveled between towns in a small twin-engine, prop-driven plane that Andy had chartered for the tour.

One night we were in the air, and the weather was not good. In fact, it was just plain terrible. A dog sled wouldn't have gone out in that weather. The plane started to ice-up, and because of that, the autopilot suddenly disengaged. Before the pilot could regain control of the plane, we rolled over and went into a dive. It didn't take long for the pilot to regain control, but during those few seconds (which seemed like an eternity), Andy and I looked at each other as if to say, "Hey, it's been great." No words came out of my mouth. My life flashed before me.

Another night we were having dinner together after a show in the Midwest, and after eating, Andy and I both went to the restroom. While we were standing in front of the urinal, some man opened the door to the men's room and his wife took a picture of Andy peeing. Andy just waved to her and said "Hi." If that had been Mr. Sinatra, I hate to think what would have happened. It would have been tabloid headlines for weeks. I still see Andy from time to time. He'll always be one of my favorite guys.

I've been privileged to work with these people and I have learned much from all of them. There have also been a few not-so-well-known performers with whom I have worked who deserve mention because they have afforded me the opportunity to continue developing my craft. They are, in most cases, as equally talented as the entertainers mentioned above, but never reached their level of celebrity. They include the great singing impressionists Bob Anderson and Bill Acosta. Both of these men are great singers as well as wonderful impressionists. The truly great musicians that have inspired me are too numerous to list, but among them is Sid Cooper whose contribution to me has been enormous. Those great people were an inspiration to me and have played an important role in my life.

CHAPTER

32

Great Arrangers

During my career, I have had the great fortune of working with, and becoming friends with, some of the greatest arrangers of all time. They were inspired by the great American composers and their music will be around for decades.

I remember when I met Nelson Riddle for the first time in Las Vegas. I was hired to play piano for a dance that featured the Nelson Riddle Orchestra. The musicians were all Las Vegas players, and Nelson sent his son Chris to Las Vegas to rehearse the music. Nelson came in for the engagement and to conduct the orchestra. Naturally, all of the music to be played was written and/or arranged by Nelson. This was long before I started working for Mr. Sinatra. I was in awe of Nelson Riddle.

All through the evening's performance, Nelson kept looking in my direction with what I thought was a pained look on his face. Every time I would play something that I thought was good, he would look my way and frown. I was crushed. By the end of the evening I was so depressed from thinking I had displeased Nelson Riddle, that all I wanted to do was to sneak out and go find a job selling shoes. Then, as I was leaving, the man who had hired me stopped me. He said that Nelson Riddle had asked him to tell me how much he had liked my interpretation of his music. The looks Nelson was giving me were looks of approval that I had misinterpreted as looks of disdain. The wave of relief that swept over me after hearing the good news is still fresh in my memory. I came to know Nelson better during my time with Mr. Sinatra and found him to be a wonderful man with a very dry sense of humor. He was truly one of the great arrangers of all time.

I first met Billy May while we were recording *Trilogy*. Mr. S had selected Billy to do the first of the three records, entitled *The Past*. Billy was a fun guy with a wonderful sense of humor. It showed prominently in his music. I also got to work with him when he did some arrangements for Andy Williams. Billy was most noted for his big band arrangements, but listening to *Trilogy*, it becomes immediately obvious that his talent extended to large orchestrations as well. He was another of the greats.

On the other hand, Billy Byers was, to my thinking, the best of the big-production-number arrangers. He could do Broadway shows as well as swinging big band songs. I think that, when an arrangement was needed that would cater to big productions with singers and dancers, there was no better man than Billy Byers.

Another great was Don Costa. Don was a veritable genius. His ability to create moods with complex harmonic interludes, and his sensitivity to the needs of singers, was unparalleled. His writing for the likes of Eydie Gorme, Steve Lawrence, Frank Sinatra, and many others has never been equaled, in my humble opinion. Don was loved and admired by everyone who knew him, and he was especially revered by fellow musicians. Don idolized Frank Sinatra, and when he was in his presence, he became a wide-eyed fan. I would always remind Don of who he was and what he meant to the rest of us, because I hated to see such a giant talent be so subservient to anyone, even Mr. Sinatra. I learned a lot from working with Don. He was generous with his talent, and he helped me to be a better musician. There were few who could match him.

Gordon Jenkins was a special man to me. I adored him for his kindness and generosity. He gave me perhaps the best lesson in conducting that I have ever received from anyone. Gordon's writing was unique in many ways. He was not what one would call a swinger, but his knowledge of the orchestra and its potential for colors and beauty was among the best ever. Gordon was also a composer of great renown. Among his many compositions is the great song, "This Is All I Ask." He composed and arranged the entire third record of *Trilogy* entitled *The Future*. His life's work would take forever to list—it's that extensive.

Harry Sukman is an unfamiliar name to many people, but not to those of us in the music industry. He was a great concert pianist and one of Hollywood's most prolific composers. In 1960, he was awarded an Academy Award for his score for the film *Song Without End*, which was the life story of Franz Liszt. He also wrote the scores for more than two hundred episodes of various television series. I was sent to Harry by Mr. Sinatra to work with him on a project that featured me as a solo pianist as part of the Sinatra show. What an honor! Harry immediately took me under his wing, and we became fast friends. He helped me in many ways. He's been gone since 1984, but in April 2005, the University of Hartford—in association with Harry's daughter, Susan Sukman-McCray—dedicated a foyer to his memory. Susan donated Harry Sukman's Steinway piano, and the foyer serves as an inspiration to the students of the Hartt School of Music at the university. As part of the dedication, I was invited to conduct the Hartford Symphony Orchestra in a concert of Harry Sukman's music. He was an important part of the Hollywood scene during his life.

Nick Perito is one of my favorite conductor/arrangers. Watching him work with Steve & Eydie, Perry Como, and others taught me a great deal about conducting and handling an orchestra. His writing is among the best. If you ever listen to the arrangements he wrote for Steve & Eydie, you will know what

I mean. I am proud to call him my friend.

It would be impossible to talk about the great arrangers and not mention Sammy Nestico. Sammy is one of the most prolific of all the writers. His work appears in the books of many great singers and big bands, as well as in the libraries of many school systems across America. He has written extensively for the academic community. His credits include Count Basie's Band, Frank Sinatra, and so many others that it would be impossible to list them all. To me, the name Sammy Nestico and the word "swinging" are one and the same. I have never played arrangements that swing as hard as Sammy's yet are still examples of intricate and complex harmonic writing. When I was working with the great Robert Farnon, he told me that of all the American arrangers, Sammy Nestico was his favorite. That is the equivalent of Albert Einstein saying that someone has a sharp mind. Sammy is a good friend and a great gentleman.

Then there was Robert Farnon. He was undoubtedly one of the most respected arrangers in the world. He is the envy of every arranger I know. I had the pleasure of working with him on three recording sessions in London over the years. What I learned from this man could not have been paid for in a hundred years. His concept of orchestra colors and his use of the instruments is pure genius. He has allowed me to be his friend, and he has been a father figure to me since I first met him in 1984. Talent like his comes along maybe once in a generation; it must be studied and appreciated.

To have known such great men and to have been able to call them my friends is something that defies description. If I have learned anything from those great arrangers, it is that one must never stop learning about the art of music. A musician should not simply envy what these great arrangers possess, but rather they must study these artists and try to ascend to their level no matter how impossible that might be.

CHAPTER
33
Funny People and Tough Guys

In addition to all the musicians I have known, I have been fortunate enough to get to know some of the funniest people who ever lived. I was truly blessed to hear some of the jokes and listen to the laughter that they brought to the stage.

For example, there was Milton Berle. I had watched Uncle Miltie's *Texaco Star Theater* when I was kid, and I couldn't appreciate his humor as a child. As an adult I got to work with him, and I found him to be a comic genius. For Frank Sinatra's sixty-fifth birthday party, Milton Berle was asked to be the emcee and I was asked to accompany him on the piano.

One peculiar thing about Milton was the way he dealt with musicians at rehearsal. I think he was attempting to convince musicians that he knew more about music than perhaps he did. He would stop the orchestra midway through a song, turn to the pianist, and say, "Stop, stop, that's not right...no, no start again." Then, the musician would replay it, in exactly the same way, and he would say, "Now you've got it. That's perfect. Absolutely perfect." I had always heard about this, and when he did it to me during our rehearsal, I played it again exactly as I had before and sure enough he said, "Yeah, Vinnie, that's correct now."

Then there was Mel Brooks. I didn't know Mel Brooks until meeting him one day in London. I was there to work with

Pia, and had just arrived at the airport. There was a message waiting for me from Tino Barzie, and I was instructed not to go directly to the hotel, but to meet Pia and Tino nearby for dinner first. As I was getting out of the cab at a restaurant, someone tapped me on the shoulder and asked if he could take my bags. It was Mel Brooks. Pia, Tino, and I then had a wonderful and funny dinner together with Mel and wife, Anne Bancroft.

I loved George Burns. Morty Jacobs was George Burns' pianist for years, and I loved to see them perform together. They were both getting on in years. George was probably ninety or so; Morty was considerably younger, but also quite senior. They were both in great shape for their ages. George would begin his show with a monologue that he did off the top of his head. In fact, he did his entire show without cue cards. When he would occasionally make a mistake, he would just look at the audience and say, "What do you want? I'm an old man."

At a certain point in the show he would ask Morty to bring him another drink. Morty would bring it over and place it on a table next to George. George would then get up and help Morty back to the piano. Burns made getting old funny.

I was conducting one night at the Riviera for both Burns and Pia. My parents were in the audience. After the show George invited my parents to come backstage. He said, "Let's get a photographer," one came from the casino to take a picture of him with my parents. As they were leaving, George grabbed my mother's arm, pulled her aside, and said, "Next time you come to see me, come alone." It made her evening.

Red Buttons was really funny and a nice person as well. I liked working with him because he always acknowledged my presence onstage. Red Buttons didn't make fun of people—as other comedians like Don Rickles did—he made fun of life. I remember that his take on getting old included lines like these: "Old is when you're complimented on your alligator shoes, and you're walking barefoot"; "You know you're old when the doctor stops taking X-rays and just holds you up to the light"; "Old is when you rent a porno flick, and it's *Debbie Does Dialysis*"; and "Old is when a beautiful woman crosses your path and your pacemaker opens your garage door." After one of those lines he might turn to me and say, "That's *old*, isn't it Vinnie?" Red was a real funny comedian.

Then there is Charlie Callas. Charlie Callas not only *is* funny, he *looks* funny. After Mr. Sinatra's longtime opener, Pat Henry, passed away, Charlie Callas became Sinatra's opening act. Once we were flying in a helicopter from New York City to Hartford, Connecticut, and Charlie decided to do his "Playmate of the Month" routine. He assumed different centerfold poses and recited stupid lines (like those that would appear beneath centerfold pictures) that were just plain ridiculous. Everybody started laughing, Mr. Sinatra was almost rolling on the floor, and Charlie wouldn't stop. The two pilots couldn't hold the helicopter still. If Charlie was any funnier, they would have to lock him up.

One of the comedians that shared the bill with Pia Zadora was Norm Crosby. He has become a great friend of mine. Norm is the sweetest man in the world, and when we were on the road together we hung out quite a bit.

Norm is famous for using malapropisms (funny mispronunciations and misuses of selected words). My former father-in-law was a simple man from upstate New York and he sometimes used malapropisms inadvertently. He and my mother-in-law came to live near us in Las Vegas. One day he wanted tickets to see Siegfried and Roy, but he asked for tickets to see Sigmund and Freud. I told Norm, and he liked it so much he used it in his act.

Norm had a war injury caused by a shell that went off near him, resulting in almost a complete loss of hearing. One time we were in the middle of an outdoor show in Cincinnati, and the batteries went dead in his hearing aid. He couldn't hear the audience's reaction, and even worse, he could feel the vibration of his voice but not really hear what he was saying. Norm finished his act and told me he wasn't sure if he was speaking correctly or not. The only thing he could tell was that the audience was laughing because he saw smiles on their faces.

Another time when we were staying in Boston, a fire alarm went off at about three a.m. We were advised to evacuate. Norm takes his hearing aid out at night, so I went to the room and was beating on the door, but he never woke up. Thankfully, the fire turned out to be a false alarm.

Phyllis Diller always brought the house down when performing in Las Vegas. A lot of people don't know this, but Phyllis is a trained classical pianist. Would you believe it? During the middle of her crazy show, she would sit down and play a classical number while I was conducting the orchestra. Mouths would drop. She was really very good.

Totie Fields was one of the funniest women to ever live. She was the first true celebrity for whom I played after coming to Las Vegas. When I was working at the Dunes, it was the policy of the hotel to close the Casino de Paris show for two weeks each December in order to refurbish the sets and the costumes and to rehearse any new acts that might be joining the show. During that period, the hotel would bring in a headliner and Totie was chosen the first year I was there. For the Casino de Paris show, the band was in a balcony, high up to the left of the stage—but was referred to as "the pit." We were moved out of our pit and onto the stage for Totie's show. When she came to rehearsal, the first thing she said was, "Look at this! They took you guys out of the pit and put you into big time f**king show biz." We had a great two weeks with her.

A few years later, when I was playing in one of the lounges at Caesars, Totie was walking through the lounge with Billy Weinberger, who was at that time the president of Caesars

Palace. She stopped to talk to me and she told Mr. Weinberger to be sure and take good care of me because I was special to her. What a nice gesture! I think it helped because Mr. Weinberger was always good to me during his tenure with Caesars.

You can't talk about Las Vegas comics without mentioning Buddy Hackett. He could make you laugh even if he just read from the phone book. Buddy was one of the funniest men ever and was also extremely off-color. However, Billy Weinberger hated anything dirty. Buddy signed a one-year contract with Caesars, and Billy went to Buddy's dressing room before his first show and begged him to be clean. Buddy came onstage and told of the conversation. He told the audience that Billy said, "Be clean, be clean, be clean." Buddy then said: "I've taken six f**king showers. This is as clean as I'm going to get." Buddy finished the year at Caesars and was fired the minute his contract was over.

I remember one of Buddy's favorite jokes was:

I do not sit in judgment about people's sexual prefer-
ences. I have no problems with gays, bless them, but
when they break the law, they break the law. Just a
few days ago on Santa Monica Boulevard, these three
gay guys grabbed this girl, two held her down, and
the third one did her hair. That's not right.

Buddy was one of comedy's real legends.

I worked a lot with Pat Henry. He was the opening comic for Frank Sinatra for many, many years. Pat once told me a funny story about an episode during that time: One time after getting off the road with Mr. Sinatra, Pat said he was happy to get back to his home in Palm Springs. That night after dinner, Mr. Sinatra called him and asked him to come to the airport and take a quick ride in a new plane one of his friends had just purchased. Pat didn't want his wife to know he was going out to meet the old man, so he told his wife he was "going out for cigarettes." He went to the airport, got on the plane with Mr. Sinatra and a couple of his cronies, and they decide to fly to Paris. Pat returned three days later. His wife wanted to know what took so long. Pat said, "They didn't have the brand I was looking for."

I have nothing but the highest respect for Jerry Lewis as a man and as an artist. Jerry called me in 2003 to go to Barcelona, Spain, where he was being honored and was to perform with the Barcelona Symphony. He asked me to conduct and play piano for him. I had gotten to know Jerry casually over the years by virtue of being with Sinatra and by performing several times on the MDA Jerry Lewis Telethon, but I had never had the chance to work directly for him. He is a man of unlimited talent and intellect. He is gracious and generous, but he does insist on perfection from himself and those around him, or so it seems to me. I wish more people were like him in that regard.

Every impressionist reveres Rich Little. His regular pianist is Chuck Hoover, but I get to work with Rich from time to time when Chuck is unavailable. Rich and I have become buddies over the years, and I have seen firsthand how talented he is. It all started when Frank Sinatra took a shine to him. Rich did many shows with us while I was with Sinatra, including a gala in Ottawa, Canada, Rich's hometown. I think the entire city was there that night, including all his friends and relatives. I know how proud Rich was to bring Frank Sinatra to Ottawa.

Once, Rich was doing a benefit performance in Palm Springs with Mr. Sinatra and former President Gerald Ford was in the audience, sitting directly in front of the stage. Mr. Sinatra and I were standing on the side of the stage waiting to go on after him. President Ford had been the object of many jokes related to his supposed tendency to trip or fall down. In other words, he was perceived as a klutz.

Without anyone's knowledge, Rich had a lectern built out of Styrofoam and had it painted and placed onstage. It had the presidential seal, and looked as if it was handmade and had cost a zillion bucks. During his act, Rich did impressions of certain presidents, including his famous Richard Nixon impression. He used the lectern as a president would when giving a speech. When he got to his Gerald Ford impression, Rich leaned against the lectern, it collapsed, and Rich fell to the floor directly in front of President Ford. The audience went wild, President Ford laughed uncontrollably, and Mr. Sinatra literally fell to the floor. That was the best practical joke I have ever witnessed in my life.

Rich looks great for all the years he's been in show business. He says, "The secret to looking young is to only hang around people who look older than you." That's Rich!

I still work with Joe Piscopo, who does an outstanding Frank Sinatra impression and includes it in his performance. In 1978, when I was in New York to perform with Mr. Sinatra at Carnegie Hall, my wife and I entered our hotel room after the show and I turned on the TV. As the picture came up on the tube, there was Joe Piscopo doing his famous Sinatra impersonation on *Saturday Night Live*. Almost immediately, I hear him say my name, along with Nelson Riddle and Don Costa, as Mr. Sinatra's music directors and arrangers. I asked my wife if I had really heard what I thought I'd heard or was I imagining it. I hadn't been with Mr. Sinatra that long, and I couldn't imagine that anyone had noticed. But Joe had noticed, and the next day he called me at my hotel and invited me to come to NBC to meet him and hang out. When I went to NBC the next day, I met not only Joe but also Eddie Murphy. Joe and I have been close friends ever since. We work together whenever Joe does his big band show. We were invited to perform at the Republican National Convention in September 2004.

Don Rickles is something else. I have come to know Don Rickles over the years, and I consider him a friend. He offered me the job as pianist for his show once, and I was tempted to take it, but I really wanted to stick to the singers because they presented the greatest musical challenge. Don is one of the funniest and (believe it or not) nicest people in the business. He could make Sinatra laugh like few others. One night Don and I arrived at the Golden Nugget in Atlantic City at the same moment. As we both got out of our respective cars, he looked at me and said, "Well look who's here, Sinatra's idol."

At the Caesars Palace celebration of Mr. Sinatra's fortieth year in show business, which was one of the most memorable shows I did with him, Don Rickles had Mr. S literally on the floor with lines like, "Frank, it's over, the voice is shot."

There is a classic Sinatra-Rickles story that Frank Sinatra and Don Rickles each told me on separate occasions. Early in Don's career, he was having dinner with a young lady when Sinatra walked into the restaurant with some friends and sat down to have dinner. Don's date was very excited to see Frank Sinatra in person, and she told Don how she would love to meet him but knew that it was hardly likely. Don told the girl that he and Mr. S were good friends and that he would see to it that she met him. Of course, Don was just bragging to impress the young lady. He had met Mr. Sinatra before, but he was not yet what you would call "a friend." Don got up and went to Mr. Sinatra's table and, as politely and humbly as he could, asked Mr. Sinatra if he could possibly stop at his table and say hello when he was leaving, if it wasn't too much of an imposition. When Frank Sinatra finished his dinner, he indeed went to Don's table and said, "Hi Don, how are you?" Don merely looked up at him and said, "Frank, can't you see we're eating?" I can't imagine anybody but Rickles getting away with that. Mr. S thought that was one of the funniest things that ever happened to him.

I remember when Mr. Sinatra held a benefit show for the University of Nevada, Las Vegas, at the Aladdin Theatre for the Performing Arts. He had all his friends perform, including Danny Thomas. He ran a tight ship for the show, and asked everybody to do twenty minutes, no more. Danny went on and did forty minutes. He thought he was on a roll and worked the crowd, oblivious to the schedule. Frank Sinatra and I were in the wings. As Danny came offstage and passed us Mr. S said, "Thanks, Danny, but f**k you." Danny got the message.

I was the house pianist at Caesars when Flip Wilson appeared there. I used to love watching Flip perform the repertoire of characters that he had created: Geraldine Jones, blue-collar man Marvin Latimer, everyday man Freddie Johnson, the flamboyant Reverend Leroy (pastor of the Church of What's Happening Now), and Sonny, the White House janitor. They were all hilarious.

Don Costa was Flip's conductor and arranger. The music portion included bringing the various characters Flip had invented on and off the stage, plus a couple of novelty tunes. Don considered the music he wrote for Flip to be "incidental music," not the type of serious arrangements that he was famous and respected for. There was even one number called "Hole at the Bottom of the Sea," which was a comedy bit where Flip sang and Don played guitar. Don confided in me that he was slightly embarrassed by the fact that he is known as a serious music arranger and it was a little beneath him to be part of this musical comedy act. Flip, however, wanted Don so badly that he made Don an offer that couldn't be refused.

I met Jonathan Winters at Mr. Sinatra's sixty-fifth birthday party in Palm Springs. The party had a western theme, and everybody showed up in cowboy outfits. Mr. Sinatra wore a cowboy hat, and Winters came dressed in a Union Soldier outfit. Jonathan came over, grabbed Mr. S by the arm and said,

"Let's get out of here, Frank, before the Indians attack. C'mon let's go, hurry up." He is one of the craziest people I have ever met.

It wasn't all laughs. Some of the people I met working in show business were pretty serious, if not scary. The entertainment business has always had its share of "tough guys." They could be agents, performers, bodyguards, club owners, or just fans. I've run into quite a few over the years.

Back in Syracuse my favorite tough guy was Dominick Bruno. Dominick was the owner of the Three Rivers Inn. Three Rivers was located about ten miles north of Syracuse (in the middle of nowhere), and it was where the major stars would appear. Unfortunately, thanks to the club's location, some nights there was more help than customers. Sometimes the band from the bar would come into the showroom to make it look like a crowd. Because of this, Dominick was a little slow paying his creditors at times. He would have to rely on his jukebox and vending machine businesses to bail him out of the hole. Many times people would come into the club looking for payment, and they would walk out with pockets full of quarters.

Even when Dom was months behind on his bills, everyone still liked him. He had that type of personality. He would give his biggest creditors front-row seats for shows like Sammy Davis Jr., Tony Bennett, or Steve & Eydie, and the creditors loved it. Drinks were on the house, they got their pictures taken with the stars, and then they would give him even more credit.

Dominick was a little guy with a certain type of charm, but he didn't appeal to everyone. For those who didn't agree with him, he had friends who could help them come over to his way of thinking. One particular night he left the club with a little too much to drink and was stopped for speeding by a local police officer. The cop, as Dom told it, stuck a flashlight in his face, and all Dom wanted to do was try to get the light out of his eyes, so he pushed the flashlight away. The officer then took him to a jail to spend the night, where he would be arraigned in the morning. Dominick said, "OK, but please don't tell anybody about it because I don't want it in the papers." He then (again in Dom's words) "went very quietly in the patrol car, was taken to jail, and spent the night in the cell." The next day he made bail and was released. That morning it was in all the papers. I'm not sure what happened to the officer, but I got the impression that after he got well again, he found a job in Detroit.

Years later, the Three Rivers Inn burned down during a particularly slow time of year. As luck would have it, some of the equipment, including a seven-foot Yamaha grand that Dominick had recently purchased, had been moved the week before to another club Dom owned in Canastota, New York. I hope he had insurance. I liked Dominick. He was a friend to all the local musicians. May he rest in peace.

One tough guy I remember in particular was Louie Scungile. That was not his real name, because I sure as hell am not going to put his real name in this book. I met him after I started working in Las Vegas with Mr. Sinatra. Louie had been, in his younger days, a man who had the respect of his peers, and was a big Sinatra fan. He saw me as a young upcoming Italian boy who had made good as Mr. Sinatra's music director. Louie was always kind to me, and I liked him…at a distance.

A few years after leaving Mr. Sinatra's employ, I was acting as music director for Paul Anka. I hadn't seen or heard from Louie in a very long time, when one day I got a call from him while we were working in Las Vegas. He asked me if I remembered Joey Boombatz (definitely not a real name either), who was a mutual acquaintance, and told me that Joey wanted to see Paul's show while we were in Las Vegas.

I did remember Joey. I remembered his reputation as well. I told Louie that I would do whatever I could for him regarding getting tickets to the show. Shortly after my conversation with Louie, I received a call from a gruff-sounding man with a New Jersey accent. He told me that he "represented Joey" and wanted me to be sure to secure four tickets to Friday night's performance. I told him I would make the arrangements and call him back. He told me that he did not have a telephone, and he would instead call me back the next day. That was Thursday, and I called my people to get the tickets for the night he wanted. Later that same day I was called and told that Paul Anka was sick and would have to cancel Friday night's show.

The next morning I was called by the hotel ticket office and asked if I wanted to reschedule the tickets for a different date because of the Friday night cancellation. I asked them to reschedule them for Saturday night. I had no way to contact Joey's "representative," so I had to wait until he called me. He phoned me that afternoon, and I explained what had happened. I told him that I had rescheduled Joey's tickets for Saturday night. He told me he would relay the message to Joey and get back to me.

He called me back an hour later and told me that Joey was "very disappointed" because he had to leave Las Vegas Saturday and wouldn't be around for the show. Before hanging up, however, he told me that Joey had said that I was "*not* to worry," (like it was my fault the Friday night show had cancelled) and that he would call me the next time they were in Las Vegas. I was relieved. I called Louie and told him what had transpired. When I told Louie that I had rescheduled Joey for Saturday night and that he could not attend, Louie (never one for a lot of words) simply said, "Then f**k him." Connected guys had their own way of handling things.

I have met a lot of characters in my time, but none so unique as Sonny Avarona from Philadelphia. Sonny had a very successful scrap metal business. I met Sonny in Atlantic City while appearing there with Mr. Sinatra. Sonny was a huge Sinatra fan, and he always wanted to pursue a singing career. At one time he converted an old church in south Philly into a nightclub where he could sing and feature other entertainment. It was very successful until a violent event took place, which forced him to close.

To his credit, Sonny never lost sight of his dream of becoming a professional singer, and he continued to pursue it. One night while in Atlantic City with Andy Williams, I was walking through one of the hotels when I heard a group performing in one of the lounges. I couldn't see the lounge from where I was, but I could hear someone singing Sinatra songs with a small group. As I followed the sound of the music to find the lounge, I heard the pianist play a passage from a song that was identical to what I had played on the recording of that same song with Mr. Sinatra. When I got to the lounge, I was amazed to find Sonny Avarona appearing as the headliner in that lounge. He was doing a tribute to Frank Sinatra, featuring many of the songs that I had recorded with Mr. Sinatra. After that, Sonny was booked in Las Vegas at the Tropicana. At his request, I hired musicians to play for him while he was in Las Vegas. Sonny's gone now, but I admired one of the tough guys living out his dream.

Tough guys were always a part of the entertainment business. Louie the Lip, Tommy the Clam, Knuckles, Snake-Eyes, and many other guys with just one name made up a lot of the front-row tables at a lot of the shows. I made up these names, not because I fear repercussion, but because they never liked visibility. They were customers. Some became friends. But it was easier being on the stage than at the tables.

CHAPTER

34

Steve & Eydie

I have had the pleasure of working with Mr. and Mrs. Steve Lawrence for the past few years. Professionally known as Steve Lawrence and Eydie Gorme, or simply Steve & Eydie, I think they are the best singing and comedy team of all time. I am happy to be their orchestra conductor on their current tour, as well as their friend.

They are two kids from New York. Their musical backgrounds are in different genres: Eydie's is with the big bands, and Steve, whose father was a cantor, had an early career as a rock-era teen idol. However, they have appeared side by side since 1960.

Had they not married and become Steve & Eydie, I believe each of them would have become huge stars, but they chose to stay together and perform together. They're devoted to one another and have a great time together.

Seven or eight years ago I got a call from Elliot Weisman. In addition to being Mr. Sinatra's manager, he managed Liza Minnelli, as well as Steve & Eydie. Elliot called to ask if I would be interested in being Steve & Eydie's pianist. Terry Trotter was still their pianist at the time, and he had become a friend of mine. I was also very busy with Tony Bennett, so I thanked him but declined the offer. They hired another very good pianist, Bob Alberti, who had played with Bob Hope for years. Nevertheless, Steve & Eydie decided after a while to look again into having me come onboard.

In 2002, I was working in Las Vegas at a casino with a talented singer by the name of Frankie Randall. He was a popular recording artist in the 1960s. I knew Frankie because he was a friend of Frank Sinatra's, and they used to spend a good amount of time together. Frankie Randall became the entertainment director for the Golden Nugget, and when I was conducting for Frank Sinatra, that was one of the places we performed.

One night Steve & Eydie showed up in the audience. I wasn't surprised to see them there, as I had known them casually over the years. They had previously seen me perform with Sinatra and with Eddie Fisher. I didn't know this till later on, but they had come this time specifically because they wanted to see me work.

Three weeks later they called and offered me the job as their pianist and conductor. This time, I jumped at the opportunity. I am glad I did because theirs is probably one of the finest shows in the industry. In fact, they are unquestionably the best showroom act there is right now. Even though they have both grown older, neither of them has lost any vocal acuity. They both still sing like young people.

The first engagement I had with them was in Cerritos, California. I had the advantage of working with the orchestra from L.A. I already knew most of the musicians from all the years I'd been performing. These were many of the same people I knew from when I'd recorded with Mr. Sinatra.

Still, I had to learn Steve & Eydie's show in a hurry. They sent me an audiotape from one of their past performances, which, of course, only included those songs they'd chosen for that particular show. Their repertoire list is vast. They have a home in Las Vegas, so I was also able to go to their house and work at their piano.

However, no matter how diligently a performer works and how much attention they pay, he or she never really learns a show until it's performed. When we did the show, I thought that it had gone quite well, and I was relatively happy with it, but I knew I could do better. The performances I'm able to give them now are far superior to that opening night. But Steve was ecstatic. He came up to me after the show, kissed me on the cheek, and thanked me.

I think the reason he was so enthusiastic was because I had solved the problem they had been experiencing with their previous conductor. I think my solution had something to do with the tip that Gordon Jenkins had given me years earlier, about never taking my eyes off the performers, and following them closely. That was extremely important to Eydie because she's very dramatic when she sings. They are both magnificent singers, and they need to have the conductor follow them precisely in order to keep the orchestra in sync with them. One reason for this need is because they don't sing the songs the same way every time. They sing their songs the way they feel about them at that moment, the way a true artist does.

That was Mr. Sinatra's method, too, and I was also able to satisfy him. Still, I was surprised by Steve's enthusiastic reaction that night, because I knew that, even though I had worked very hard at that show, I was capable of doing a far better job, it was just going to take some time.

The bond and the friendship that has developed between us is not only musical, but it is extremely personal. I consider them—and I think they consider my present wife, Annette, and me—very close personal friends, as well as associates.

The caliber of their music is as good as it gets—and I'm not exaggerating. They have arrangements by the greatest arrangers that ever lived. I believe their music is as good as Frank Sinatra's was, and it is as good as anybody's in the business has ever been. It is the icing on the cake to be able to maintain that level of excellence for two great singers.

Mr. Sinatra used to say to me, "When we're not great, we'd better be damn good." That's the same premise from which Steve & Eydie work. They are perfectionists, as well they should be. And it's good for me, because whenever I take extra time in a rehearsal to make sure the orchestra does things the way I know they should be done—the way Steve & Eydie want it done—there's never any argument. Unfortunately, I have found that for some performers it's not that important to get things exactly right. Some of them have the attitude that they just want to get through the rehearsal.

Eydie and I always do at least one number in the show where it's just the piano and her. Lately, we've been doing one song we haven't performed in a long, long time, because it's not an easy song to sing, and it's not an easy song to accompany. It's "Send in the Clowns," from A Little Night Music, composed by Stephen Sondheim.

I used to do "Send in the Clowns" with Mr. Sinatra. Eydie is the only one I've ever done that song with who sings it as well as Mr. S and seems to understand what it means. She understands something about the Great American Songbook that young singers never seem to grasp, with a couple of exceptions. These songs are not just words put to music. These songs are life experiences put to music. "Send in the Clowns" has a specific meaning. If you've ever been to the circus and something goes wrong, what do they do? They send in the clowns. It is a love story about two people whose relationship is falling apart. And Eydie fully understands this.

When we started doing this song, it just grabbed the audience. One night, however, she had a mental block. She couldn't remember the words. And the way she handled it was so ingenious. In fact, we all made a funny thing out of it. Steve was standing in the wings, and he starts yelling to her, "What's the matter, can't you remember?" And the audience can hear this. (He's a natural comedian; had he not been a singer, he would have been one of the great comics.)

She sat for two or three minutes on the stool, playing with the lyric, until finally I opened up the book with the lyrics in it and said, "Here they are!" and handed her the lyrics, and she said, "Oh, yeah!" And then we went back into the mood and she sang the song, and the audience came to their feet. It was just one of those moments. You see, in order to take a problem and turn it into a positive, you have to have the poise, experience, and intelligence to know how to deal with it.

With Mr. Sinatra, that would happen every now and then. He'd forget a lyric, and I'd turn around and yell out the words to him, and he'd make a joke out of it. Or he'd announce the wrong song; for example, he introduced "I've Got You Under My Skin" when he should have been announcing "For Once in My Life." I could tell by what he was saying that he was introducing the wrong song, and I'd yell, "No, Boss," and he'd turn around, look at me, and make a joke to the audience about me interrupting him.

The audience loves to see this interaction. They love the real life that is missing in someone who comes out and does the same act night after night, with word after word set in stone.

The banter between Steve & Eydie—in the middle of their show when they do a bit of comedy—is always fresh. One of the unique things about them is that they can do the same comedy bit every single night, and the audience will think it's the first time they've ever done it. They are so incredibly talented at making what they do seem impromptu. They are so clever and so quick, it changes every time.

When we go out on tour, Steve & Eydie always throw a big dinner for the entire crew the night before we open. Our crew comprise of their wardrobe assistant, their personal assistant, the best sound man and the best light man with whom I have ever worked, and five musicians, including myself. The musicians, aside from me, are lead trumpet, guitar, bass, and drums, and they're augmented with an orchestra wherever we go.

Steve & Eydie are two down-to-earth people, and they never put on that Hollywood attitude. I can't think of anyone with whom I've ever worked that I enjoy not only musically, but personally, more than the two of them. In fact, we keep saying we should have gotten together years ago. It's been wonderful, and I hope the relationship will continue. Their musical expertise is beyond great.

It's truly become a family, and one of the best parts is that my wife, Annette, has also become great friends with Eydie. My wife's father, Sonny, is a retired musician who was the bandleader at the Concord Hotel in the Catskills and very well known. Annette was raised in the Catskills and grew up on the grounds of the Concord. As a result, she met many of the great entertainers that performed there.

Many of those entertainers knew her as a little girl. Pat Henry, Pat Cooper, Jackie Mason, and Buddy Hackett were among them. She used to babysit for some of the performers' children, and she once gave Buddy Hackett's son, Sandy, an ice skating lesson. Annette is also a very talented singer and growing up her idol was Eydie Gorme, just like Frank Sinatra, Oscar Peterson, and Art Tatum were mine. When I went to work for Steve & Eydie, she and Eydie hit it off like two sisters. They go shopping together, and we go out to dinner with Steve & Eydie frequently.

For Annette, it's a dream come true, because she's become close social friends with a person she idolized all her life. I'm very happy that she's had that experience, because most of the people whom I idolized as a child, and as a young man, have now become my friends, and I know what that's like.

35

There Is Nothing Like Las Vegas

You can make somewhat of a living as a musician anywhere, but to make a good living, it's easier if you live in (or near) a major metropolitan market. I could have gone to New York, Chicago, or Los Angeles, but I chose Las Vegas. I had two small boys, and I didn't want to raise them in a big city environment, where I felt they would be subject to unhealthy influences. Las Vegas was relatively small when I first moved there, and the school system was very good. The air was still clean, and the cost of living was much less than in the larger cities. In short, Las Vegas still had that small town feel.

I am glad that I decided to move to the green felt capital of the world. Las Vegas has treated me well, but man, has it changed since I arrived in 1970. It seems to continually expand and evolve by the week. When I first came to Las Vegas, the major casinos included the Sands, the Dunes, and the Desert Inn. They are all gone now. They have been imploded in spectacles that were shown on TV. The Wynn has replaced the Desert Inn. It cost $2.7 billion to build and, if you want to play golf there, the greens fees are five hundred dollars per person as this book is being written.

The Venetian now stands where the Sands used to be. In the lobby of the Venetian there is a large circle with a peach and black sunburst, and a smaller black circle in the center. Someone had found the original plans for the Sands, and saw where the stage in the showroom once was. The circle was put down indicating where Frank Sinatra once stood during his show. There is no sign. You have to ask its location unless you know where to look.

In the seventies, the Strip ended just one block south of the Tropicana. The hotel had so much land that it had its own golf course. Now the Tropicana is almost in the center of the Strip. The golf course is gone. New York, New York; MGM Grand; and Excalibur are on the other corners. In the 1970s, you could easily drive down the Strip and quickly go from casino to casino. You could get from the Flamingo all the way to downtown in about fifteen minutes. Now it takes fifteen minutes just to get from the Sahara to the Frontier, which are almost next to each other.

In Las Vegas, you can rent almost any exotic car in the world. You can rent a $130,000 Ferrari for about five hundred a day, but if you do, expect the air conditioner to be unhooked. There will be no air because you will end up going bumper-to-bumper down the Strip at ten p.m., cruising at about three miles per hour, and if the air conditioner was hooked up, the car would overheat.

When you drive down the Strip you'll see everything from a manmade volcano that explodes every half-hour to a replica of the Eiffel Tower. There is spectacle after spectacle, including the pirate battle at the Treasure Island casino (now called TI) that is held four times a night in the lagoon, in front of the main entrance. There are ninety-nine-cent shrimp cocktails at the Golden Gate casino, mega buffets in just about every casino for ten dollars, hotel pools that rival small lakes, and twenty-four-hour drive-through wedding chapels. That's the Tinsel Town side of Las Vegas that beckons tourists. It brings the gamblers in and spits them out.

I've been in Las Vegas so long that I've seen just about every side of gamblers you can imagine. I remember one night at the Thunderbird when a man playing blackjack collapsed from a heart attack and died. Nobody moved. The paramedics came and took him away, but the game never stopped. That probably wouldn't happen today, but in the old days, nothing stopped the table action.

When I was at Caesars Palace with Mr. Sinatra, I recall many players losing in the hundreds of thousands of dollars. That's why the casinos had big stars like Sinatra and Elvis. They paid for themselves many times over by virtue of the high rollers they attracted. Now they have huge shows like Celine Dion and Cirque du Soleil, and the players lose in the millions. At one time, fifty dollars was a big bet. Now it's a tip. If you have a ten-thousand-dollar line of credit, you're not a high roller—you're more like a low- to middle-income tourist with a few bucks to spend.

Frank Sinatra told me a story about a night at the Sands Hotel where he was appearing. There was a heckler in the crowd who was really annoying him, so Sinatra had someone backstage call security, and they threw the man out. At least they thought they had thrown him out. After the show, Mr. S noticed an elderly lady sitting ringside. She was crying. He went to her and asked her what was wrong. She said that some men had come and taken her husband away, and she didn't know why or where he was. It seems that security had thrown out the wrong man. Sinatra took her and found her husband sitting out by the pool completely confused. Mr. Sinatra told me that not only did he apologize profusely, but he and the Sands Hotel also picked up the cost of the old couple's complete vacation. It probably wasn't funny then, but it's funny now when you think about it.

I rarely gamble, and I don't drink at all except for some wine occasionally at dinner. If I did, I might have ended up driving a cab or waiting tables to pay back the markers, rather than playing and conducting for stars.

Because Las Vegas is one of the biggest entertainment centers in the world, there are always places for both musicians and entertainers to work. If you're a musician you can always do casual engagements, or weddings, or any number of functions held by visiting conventions. These days, more Broadway-type shows are coming to Las Vegas, and they employ from small groups to large orchestras. For example, Kevin Spacey was in town recently doing his Bobby Darin show. Celine Dion uses a small band, as do most of the production shows. The lounges are resplendent with piano duos and trios, or they feature rock bands.

There is another side to Las Vegas: the family entertainment scene. There are circus acts at Circus Circus, museums, water parks, thrill rides at the Stratosphere, and the list goes on and on. There are fun things to do without giving in to the call of the slots or the ripples of the cards. You can go to Lake Meade to water ski or to see the Hoover dam, or go swimming in the lake. You can go to Mount Charleston in the winter to ski or in summer to cool off and hike. You can take a helicopter ride to the Grand Canyon or sky dive over the desert. There are so many ways to enjoy Las Vegas; it is impossible to list all of them.

My living expenses in Las Vegas aren't too bad. My utility bills are small and the air conditioner is heavily used only in the summer. But my water bill could compare to some of the biggest heat bills I ever had in New York. Everything is relative. At least I don't need a snow blower, boots, or a heavy coat. I remember reading in the Syracuse newspaper online last year about someone who removed the snow from his roof with a snow blower. The snow blower got stuck because the snow was so high. That will never happen in Las Vegas.

Property values and taxes, although on the rise, are not nearly as high as the other major metropolitan areas around the country. People are moving to Vegas at the rate of about four thousand per month. Modest homes in the Los Angeles or San Francisco areas cost two or three times the price of a home in Las Vegas, which is why so many Californians are moving here.

CHAPTER
36

Life Has Its Moments

*"Don't let your only regrets in life be the chances
you didn't take."*
—*from the movie* Grumpy Old Men

My father once said to me that I was living the life that he had always dreamed about. What he didn't realize was that I was living a life I had *never* dreamed about. I had met and married Connie, and together we were raising two sons. I had a good job making good money. How could I have imagined what was in store for me?

I believe our lives are effected most by chances taken in a moment. I had many such moments in my life: the moment Connie and I decided we would take the chance that I could succeed as a musician and relocate to Las Vegas; the moment when I was heard by the bandleader at Caesars Palace, which led to my employment there; the moment when Mr. Sinatra decided I would be his next pianist-conductor; and the moment when Tony Bennett decided to call me. The list goes on and on. The moments arrive, and you must take the chance. You may fail, but if you don't grab at the chances as they arrive you will never know whether or not you have what it takes to succeed. You must also be prepared to fail and move on. No one can succeed at everything. Every successful life has some failures. It's how you deal with them and move forward that is a measure of your character.

There are other moments in life that leave lasting memories. Because my parents made sure that my brothers and I had musical training, I made sure my two sons were also exposed to music. My oldest son, Jeffrey, has become a fine drummer, and my youngest son, Danny, is currently playing trumpet for great stars such as Paul Anka and Neil Sedaka, just to name a few.

It seems like yesterday that they were little and I would take them to see me perform. One night I had my sons at a Sinatra show at Caesars. When Mr. Sinatra introduced me to the audience, he started out by saying, "This boy sitting at the piano is my pianist-conductor..." Later that night my oldest son said to me, "Dad, why did Mr. Sinatra call you a boy?" He couldn't understand how someone could call his old father a boy.

I remember a time when Jeff, who was then about sixteen years old, invited his mom and me to come hear him play in a rock group. Connie and I went to this funky rock club somewhere in Vegas to hear him, and when we entered we were ushered to a booth near the bandstand. The club was filled with teenagers, many of whom were young girls who had come to see the group. When the set was finished, Jeff was mobbed by five or six young girls all wanting to talk to him. When he finally was able to free himself and join us at our booth, he pointed to the girls and said to Connie and me, "Isn't it great being a musician?"

Once when Tony Bennett was appearing at the Riviera Hotel in Vegas, Tony's drummer at the time, Joe La Barbera, asked Jeff if he would play for him at Tony's rehearsal. Joe's daughter was ill and Joe needed to attend to her. Jeff was very nervous, but did it anyway. When Tony arrived at the rehearsal, he said nothing about Joe not being there and began the rehearsal. I purposely did not tell Tony that the drummer was my son, as I did not want to embarrass Jeff. About ten minutes into the rehearsal, Tony came over to me and quietly said what a good drummer this kid was. I was so proud and only then did I tell Tony that Jeff was my boy.

My son Danny is a world-class trumpet player, and I hire him whenever he is available to be in the orchestras I lead. One of life's great moments occurs each time I look up at the band and see my son sitting in the trumpet section. On occasion, the star for whom we are playing will introduce him as one of the special musicians in the band, which causes Danny much embarrassment. He thinks it's because he's my son, but in fact, it's because he plays so well.

Life's moments also include some terribly trying times. Getting fired by Frank Sinatra certainly was one of them. My father's passing was another. By far, the worst was the untimely death of my first wife, Connie, with whom I had spent thirty-three years and one week of my life. Just a few days after we returned from a working cruise to Bali and Hong Kong, she was diagnosed with lung cancer. She passed on fourteen months later. I thought my life had ceased to have any meaning. Over time and with the help of my two sons, I learned to cope and go on with life.

Four years later, another of life's moments occurred. I met Annette. It was amazing that we should end up together. She is not only a talented, but also a very beautiful woman. I truly never thought I could ever care for another woman after Connie, but Annette showed me that I could once again find love. We were married in September 2000.

Were it not for the fact that I have music in my life, I don't think I could have continued to be productive after losing Connie. Returning to my music career after Connie's death gave me something to live for. My two sons kept me from doing anything foolish, and Annette gave me a new life.

Life *does* have its moments. The bad ones come unannounced. You can't control them. You must learn to accept them and move forward. But the good ones have to be recognized, and you must act upon them if they are to be of value to you. Abraham Lincoln said, "It's not what happens to you that matters in life, it's how you handle what happens that matters."

I believe that you should never look over your shoulder and wonder if you made a wrong decision. The decisions you make can't all be right, but once they are made they're a done deal. If I had listened to all the people who told me I was crazy leaving Syracuse and moving to Las Vegas, look what I would have missed. Had I stayed in Syracuse, I would have been financially rich. Having followed my dream has not always made me a rich man monetarily, but I wouldn't trade my life's experience for all the money in the world.

CHAPTER
37
From This Moment On

I'm a lucky man. I still have a few great performers who call upon me to direct for them: Steve & Eydie, Robert Goulet, Jack Jones, Phyllis McGuire, and a few others. Granted there is not as much work today for the entertainers who sing the Great American Standards. Cabaret entertainment is mostly a thing of the past. Most present-day entertainers couldn't interest an audience for very long without visual effects and pyrotechnics. Many Las Vegas vocal acts now use lasers, computerized lights, fog machines, confetti guns, and lip-synching to do their shows.

The people for whom I have worked depend only on great music, talent, and the ability to entertain without gimmicks. In my estimation, hip-hop, rap, and heavy metal have destroyed the tradition of great American music that depended on inter-esting melodies and sophisticated lyrics. When I was young, music depicted love, romance, or the longing for a lost love. Today what passes for music often depicts violence, hatred, and sex. I have found that young people need only to be exposed to great art in order for them to recognize it as such. The problem today is the lack of availability of fine art to youngsters in schools. To make matters worse, funding for music education in public schools is on the decline.

Mr. Sinatra, had he not begun to lose his memory and suffer the fate that he did, would have become a teacher eventually. He had expressed to me many times his desire to teach in his declining years, after he couldn't sing onstage anymore. He told me that we would one day go around to the major music schools in the U.S. and give what he called master classes and teach younger musicians what his type of music was about and how to interpret it. By passing along his knowledge and experience, he felt he could perpetuate this great art form that I, and many others, refer to as the Great American Song Book. Unfortunately, he fell ill and passed on before he could make his dream come true.

I am dedicating what remains of my career to his goal. I have already gone to some schools, and I will continue to go where I am invited to try to carry out Mr. Sinatra's dream as he related it to me. A few university music schools have already asked me to present my program and give clinics. The students love it. They don't get to hear this music that often, and when they do, if they are any kind of musicians, they realize the depth that this music possesses.

I involve the students in the music I bring to them by having them rehearse and perform the music, while explaining to them the depth and sophistication of the music. I try to show them the difference between just playing the notes, and interpreting those same notes with dynamics and feeling. I also coach the voice students and try to show them how to be interpretive with the lyric, and how to use phrasing and dynamics to make the lyric more meaningful. This was the great legacy of Frank Sinatra, and I learned well from his teaching. He used to tell me that many times the singers of his day came to him for consultation, asking what it was that he did that they weren't doing. He said, "I told them, but they just didn't get it." Maybe *they* didn't get it, but I sure did.

I still see some young singers with the right idea. They need to keep singing the great songs even if it means not making as much money as they would if they sang the popular music of the day. It takes experience, it takes life, and it takes maturity to do this material really well. As they mature, the meaning of the music will become clearer to them, and if they have real talent, they will eventually succeed. Just look at Tony Bennett. Tony never wavered from his style and has perfected it to the point where he is admired and respected by both young and old.

Harry Connick Jr. and Diana Krall are two fine examples of singers-musicians who choose to embrace great music and appeal to a smaller audience rather than falling prey to commercialism. Anyone who continues to perform this music is doing a service because this music is part of American culture. It is as American as apple pie, and it is respected and revered around the world. Those performers are examples of true talents, and they will remain a force in music long after most of their contemporaries have faded into obscurity.

I want to continue performing as long as I am physically able. My love for this music will never diminish, and I continually look for young people with a passion for good music. Who knows, maybe the next Sinatra is out there somewhere. I'm going to keep looking until I find him or her, and then look out!

I came into this world as a piano player, I spent my life as a piano player, and I'm going out the same way. I have been extremely fortunate to play and conduct for some of the very best. Music has been my life. I can't imagine doing anything else.

EPILOGUE
A Look at the Music Business
as It Is Today

The music business has changed, and today the American Federation of Musicians recognizes not only the need to organize but also the need to assist all types of musicians, in all venues and all circumstances. We recognize that the part-time, casual-date musician, as well as the full-time musician, needs to be represented, and we want to increase our membership by appealing to and benefiting all types of players. We want our musicians to be treated fairly, paid fairly, and increase their opportunities for better work. This is one of the main agendas I am currently working on.

—Tom Lee, current president
of the American Federation of Musicians

This book was put together by two friends who have spent many years working in the music industry. Bob Popyk has worked in and studied the business, promotional, and retail side of the industry for more than forty years. His monthly columns in Music Trades and International Musician help guide professional musicians who are trying to make their dreams come true. Vincent Falcone's story of success as a professional musician is told through this book. Still, the book would be incomplete without including their thoughts about the music industry of today and some advice for aspiring musicians.

Vincent Falcone and the Entertainment Side of Music

The music business has changed radically over the years. Clubs are using less live music, big bands are becoming a thing of the past, and digital technology is replacing musicians. Downloading music from the Internet has caused CD sales to slump. Much of the music today has gone from understandable lyrics and musically-correct content to loud unintelligible noise. Obscenities and crotch-grabbing seem to be a part of mainstream performances of a lot of today's music. MTV and VH-1 should come with a warning label. I think those channels have been detrimental to the morality of youth in this country. It is becoming tougher to make a decent living playing decent music. But of course, "decent" is in the mind of the beholder.

There is a difference between music and entertainment. Music is a form of art; not all entertainment, though, is art. People who might not be educated in the technique of how great music is formed will have different ideas on what is good and what is not. Today, when some of the pop artists sing, I cannot understand the words. Is that really music or is it simply entertainment? Half the popular groups today could not play without four-hundred-watt amps, strobe lights, confetti guns, and fog. If they showed up at a gig and the electricity was off, they wouldn't be able to play. But they certainly appeal to a lot of people.

I often think we are missing out on the human side of music today. Many performers sing the same songs, the same way, performance after performance. The real star of the show then becomes their special effects.

I am a musician. I have never considered myself an entertainer. Through my career I liked playing jazz and working with big bands. I love to conduct for the country's major singers and play Las Vegas shows. I can't imagine doing anything else. I could never write and record commercials, play another ethnic wedding, join a rock group, or get involved with any type of music that I didn't like. I could never play anything that wasn't musically correct. I hate rap and think the musical tastes of the American public are deteriorating quickly. But hey, that's me. I paid my dues long ago. I get to pick and choose my work at this stage of my life. I can afford to say that because I made it the hard way. I was selling pianos and playing in some of the worst bars in the world to make a living thirty-five years ago. I played my share of strip clubs, gay bars, American Legion halls, wedding gigs, joints where you wonder if you're going to get paid at the end of the night, and bars where you get paid by check and then hope it clears the bank. I've played basements, speakeasy type "connected" joints, and places where it was tough just to get a breath of fresh air. They were all learning experiences.

Musicians who think they can go from the bottom to the top, without climbing all the steps along the way, may be very disappointed. Musicians today must take the good with the bad, play different venues, or find a different line of work. There's a lot of work for musicians out there. It may not be the kind they want or like, but they have a choice. Musicians have to decide where that line of musical integrity and artistic taste is drawn. What I might consider crap could be solid gold to them. I am not going to force my musical tastes on anybody. But during my early years as a working musician, I had to play a lot of music that just didn't appeal to me at all. Some music I just couldn't get into. I still played it. I had to make a living.

Those gigs help musicians build the foundation of their career. I always thought it was easier to ask, "What tune would you like me to play?" than, "Do you want fries with that?" Playing music is fun, and the more money we make at it, the more fun it can be. If it's the type of music or gig we really want, that's a plus. Then it's a great way to earn a living.

I always wanted to be a musician first, a pianist second, and then I fell into the role of conducting third. I wanted to play good music. I wanted to make a living playing jazz, great ballads, evergreen standards, and pop hits. I wanted to play them in a manner that, to me, was musically correct. Today there are still a ton of venues that a musician can play to make a living. The word "sideman" isn't used much today, but if a musician plays in a band that backs up a major singer or entertainer, that's pretty much what they are. It can be a very rewarding career.

A musician needs to be creative and able to go after the work that is currently available. Looking back, I think I was born with the basic talent for playing the piano, but I realize it was the passion for playing that drove me throughout my career. I am still learning more about music as each day goes by. I just love to play.

Bob Popyk's Take on the Business Side

Independent "sidemen" musicians might not get rich, but they can make a decent living being musicians. It doesn't matter what the type of music is—country, folk, jazz, symphonic, blues, rock, pop, show-tunes, ethnic, middle-of-the-road, oldies, or the hundreds of genres in between. It could be for TV shows, like the bands on late night TV, movie soundtracks, or Broadway. Maybe a musician hopes to backup singers, or just travel with a name band. Whatever it is, they have to learn their craft. For a musician to be successful, they have to know their instrument inside and out. They shouldn't be satisfied with just being able to play one type of music either, and they shouldn't be satisfied with mediocrity if they want to make music a career.

Too many musicians today go out unprepared, hoping the

world will find them a living. I'm not saying they might not get lucky if they are among the best, because these things do happen. But they need to be educated as much as an engineer or an attorney. A musician today needs an overall understanding of music if he/she expect music to be his/her career.

They also need a passion for what they want to do. Passion alone, however, won't cut it. A musician needs talent as well. There are a lot of talented musicians out there with no passion for their craft, and many more musicians who are passionate about a career in music with no talent. It takes both. Musicians with both passion and talent also need something else. To work as a professional musician, a musician needs to treat music like a business. That means networking, promo kits, demo CDs, PR programs, business cards, brochures, voice mail, an office telephone and a cell phone, e-mail, a web site, and a business plan.

A successful musician today also needs a good attitude—a business attitude. Musicians can't blame things outside of their control for not getting booked. By human nature, when things start going into "tilt," musicians who want to work come up with excuses for not getting gigs. Excuses like "the economy is bad," "clubs want musicians to work for the door," "mobile DJs are putting musicians out of work," "we're in a recession," or "nobody wants to hire live musicians anymore," I hear everyday. On top of that, working musicians blame the stock market, the president, the town where they live, the competition, or the customers themselves. However, all things considered, it is easier for them to look in the mirror and see who is actually responsible for getting work.

We are the prophets of our own destinies.

To make it in the music business today, musicians need to let people know who they are as a musician. Besides honing their craft, they need to tweak their business skills. That means marketing, selling, publicizing, networking, and promoting...as well as performing.

I have found over the years that most roadblocks for getting work as a musician can be overcome. However, it isn't easy, it takes some work, and the overnight success most musicians are trying to achieve may take just a little longer than "overnight."

Vincent mentioned earlier in this book that he is a member of the American Federation of Musicians, Local 369, Las Vegas. Before that he was a member of Local 78 in Syracuse, New York. Membership not only gave him great networking opportunities and helped him get decent pay when he worked, but he also took part in the AFM Pension Fund. Any up-and-coming musician who wants to make music his/her career should be a member of the AFM. Vincent is glad that he thought about the future back then, because age has a way of creeping up. Since he had money going into the union pension fund early on, he started receiving monthly checks at age fifty, and then it doubled when he turned sixty-five. Now those checks are a substantial amount. You have to think of your future.

The music business has changed over the years. I am the first to admit it. The line between "musician" and "entertainer" keeps drawing closer, and there are more part-time musicians out there looking for full-time work.

For a musician, a journey of a hundred miles begins with the first step. If you (or somebody you know) want to play for a living, ask this question: What are you doing *right now* to reach your goal? Personal success as a professional musician is directly related to belief in yourself and your music. So, any musician's success is in his, or her, own hands. Henry Ford said, "Whether you think you can, or whether you think you can't, you're absolutely right." Amen to that.

◆◆◆